BRIGHT
NEW IDEAS

Festivals

AGES 5–11

Roger Smith

Author
Roger Smith

Editor
Linda Mellor

Assistant Editor
Rachel Mackinnon

Series designer
Joy Monkhouse

Designer
Geraldine Reidy

Illustrations
Garry Davies

Cover photograph
© 2006 Jupiter Images Corporation

Published by Scholastic Ltd,
Villiers House,
Clarendon Avenue,
Leamington Spa,
Warwickshire
CV32 5PR

Printed by Bell & Bain Ltd, Glasgow
Text © 2006 Roger Smith
© 2006 Scholastic Ltd
1 2 3 4 5 6 7 8 9 0   6 7 8 9 0 1 2 3 4 5

Visit our website at www.scholastic.co.uk

British Library Cataloguing-in-Publication Data
A catalogue record for this book is available from
the British Library.

ISBN 0-439-94487-2
ISBN 978-0439-94487-8

Acknowledgements
The publishers gratefully acknowledge permission to
reproduce the following copyright material:
The Society of Authors as the Literary Representative
of the Estate of Laurence Binyon for the use of 'For
the Fallen' by Laurence Binyon from *The Times – 21st
September, 1914* © 1914, Laurence Binyon (1914, The
Times).
Every effort has been made to trace copyright holders for
the works reproduced in this book, and the publishers
apologise for any inadvertent omissions.

Material from the National Curriculum © The Queen's
Printer and Controller of HMSO. Reproduced under the
terms of HMSO Guidance Note 8.
Material from the NNS and NLS © Crown Copyright.
Reproduced under the terms of HMSO Guidance Note 8.

Contents

Introduction

The festivals in this book have been chosen to represent a wide and varied cross-section of a range of different celebrations. There is a festival of some kind almost every month and these special days can be used as part of the framework for the school year. Some special days have specific dates, for example, Christmas Day, St George's Day and April Fool's Day, and others are celebrated on days that are determined either by the Moon or the Sun or in relation to the dates of other festivals. Some of these will include Easter, Pentecost, Pesach and Ramadan.

Religious festivals

Many of the festivals are very old and it is possible to link them to celebrations of different civilisations, such as the Romans and Celts. Many celebrations are religious and you will find festivals that are particularly relevant to Sikhs, Muslims, Jews, Hindus and Buddhists, as well as Christians. Many classes will have children from these different religions and it is always important to be sensitive to their beliefs. Treat such children as an extra resource because they may be able to tell you even more about particular festivals and how they are celebrated. There are also similarities between many religious festivals, creating opportunities to compare different beliefs, looking at how much they have in common and perhaps go some way to create a more tolerant society. Several festivals, for example, are about harvests. Many others are about light and dark and light and fire triumphing over evil. Others, such as Lent, Easter and Pentecost; and Rosh Hashana and Yom Kippur, follow on from each other in a precise and fixed progression.

Secular festivals

Some of the special days that are not religious deal with ancient activities, such as the Winter and Summer Solstices. Others celebrate famous people and events that have become fixed in the year's calendar, such as Father's Day and Mothering Sunday. Both of these particular days may also require a sensitive approach as some children may not belong to families where they have mothers or fathers.

Planning

There are many festivals that include the use of bright colours and lots of eating, dancing and singing. These happy and lively celebrations have meant that many of the suggested activities involve painting and other artwork, together with making food and, of course, eating it. If you are planning ahead, for the term or half term, look at the festivals which occur as soon as possible because some of the suggested activities require preparation before the actual day, and some of the equipment and resources might need to be collected. Others, especially where there is cooking, will need different and possibly shared equipment and more adults in the classroom because of health and safety and possibly risk assessment implications.

Using this book

Each festival covered has notes on 'Age ranges', 'Learning objectives' and 'Curriculum links'. These suggestions will work and are there to be followed. But they will probably work best if they are used by innovative and creative teachers. Do not, for example, ignore a festival just because the suggested age range doesn't fit the ages of the children in your class. Many of the activities can be adapted to fit different age ranges and, of course, once you have read the 'Background', you may well be able to think of many more activities to do. In fact, what you ask the children to do can be as creative as you like. The activities in the 'What to do' section can be expanded or changed. What is important is that the children are as interested and as creative as possible.

To sum up, all the suggested activities are flexible. Most of the festivals can stand alone to be used as single lessons with relatively specific objectives. Others can be used as part of a wider series of lessons and may be fitted into different areas of the curriculum such as history, religious education, design and technology, and art and design. They are also flexible enough to be adapted to suit different styles of teaching. They will, for example, promote discussion; some of the activities can be used for homework; there are written activities and many also involve research, artwork and designing and making. Differentiation in many festivals is by outcome. This means more able children will have the opportunity to extend their work and to produce more detailed end products. Less able children will, of course, need support, especially where there is writing, but there are opportunities within each festival for children of all abilities to succeed.

But best of all, work on many of the festivals should lead to lively and colourful displays that will excite and interest children. Hopefully, the activities will make them want to discover more about the complex world they live in and understand some of the many traditions and beliefs that shape the world in which they will grow up.

CHAPTER 1

Autumn
September to November

AGE RANGE 5–7

LEARNING OBJECTIVES
To understand the significance of 'harvest' in
Britain and to recognise ways of celebrating it.

CURRICULUM LINKS
Science: QCA Unit 1B 'Growing plants' – to
name plants that we grow for food; Unit 2A
'Health and growth' – to understand that we
eat different kinds of food.
Design and technology: QCA Unit 1C 'Eat
more fruit and vegetables' – to understand
that a wide variety of fruit and vegetables are
available.

Harvest

What you need
A variety of harvest fruits and vegetables, such as: corn, marrow,
carrot, potato, leek and onion; a bag; carrot, leek and onion
seeds; copies of 'Harvest scones' photocopiable page 25;
ingredients for the harvest scones.

Background
The tradition of celebrating a successful harvest is
very old and held in many countries. As well as
the ceremonies and celebrations, it is also about
thanking God for the food that the harvest provides.
Harvest festival is usually held towards the end of
September close to the full harvest moon.

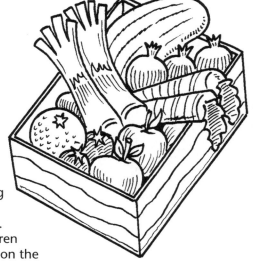

What to do
● Explain that 'harvest' is all about celebrating the
gathering of the food that farmers have grown during
the year.
● Put the fruits, vegetables and the seeds in the bag.
Take the vegetables out one by one and ask the children
what each one is. Write the names of each vegetable on the
whiteboard, or have a label to place alongside each one.
● Take out a few of the carrot and leek seeds and ask the
children what they think they are.
● Explain that the seeds have to be planted. Discuss what this means and what the best
conditions are for seeds to grow into the vegetables and fruits that they eat.
● If your school is having a harvest festival explain what it will be like and how the
festival celebrates that what has been grown can now be shared and eaten.
● Talk about the traditional celebrations of harvest suppers with geese and apples,
decorating churches with food and leaves, making corn dollies and how in some villages
church bells are rung and horses and carts are decorated with flowers and ribbons.
● Many farmers used to make bread and cakes out of the flour from the wheat.
● Check with parents and carers for any food allergies or dietary requirements, then
make the harvest scones (photocopiable page 25) have as many adults working with
the children as possible. Show the children the ingredients separately. Explain where the
flour (wheat), sugar (beet or cane) and raisins (grapes) come from and that they are all
part of the harvest.

Differentiation
Some children will need help when making the harvest scones – especially when adding
the milk. Very able children can write about different customs and find designs for corn
dollies and make them.

Rosh Hashana

AGE RANGE 7–11

LEARNING OBJECTIVES
To understand what the Jewish New Year means and how it is celebrated.

CURRICULUM LINKS
PSHE and citizenship: KS2 2e – to reflect on spiritual and cultural issues; 2i – to appreciate the range of religious and ethnic identities in the United Kingdom.

What you need
Sliced apples; honey; writing and drawing/painting materials.

Background
Rosh Hashana is the festival marking the first and second days of the Jewish New Year, when Jewish people look back on the past year and think about what they have achieved. It is celebrated in September or October. A great deal of time is spent in the synagogue during this festival, asking forgiveness for the sins of the past year. Rosh Hashana begins with a ram's horn (called a shofar) being blown like a trumpet. This is the signal for everyone in the synagogue to think about the past year. The ten-day festival ends with Yom Kippur (see page 9).

What to do
● Talk about when and how New Year in Britain is celebrated. Explain when Rosh Hashana is celebrated and that it is based on a different calendar.
● Tell them that Rosh Hashana is different because it is a religious festival and that much time is spent in the synagogue asking for forgiveness for the sins of the past year.
● Offer the children slices of apple and let them dip them in honey and eat them. As they are doing this, explain to them that after the service on the first evening of the festival a special meal is eaten – including apples dipped in honey.
● Discuss with the children their responses to these questions that are asked during the festival:
    1. What is the most meaningful thing in my life?
    2. Who means the most to me and how often do I let them know it?
    3. What are the most significant things I have achieved during the past year? (For example, winning a football competition.)
    4. What do I hope to achieve next year and in my life generally?
● Ask them to draw, paint or write about their answers to some or all of the questions. If they have things that are very precious to them, they could include them in a display.

Differentiation
Some children should only choose one of the questions to answer and will need support with their writing.

AGE RANGE 7–11

LEARNING OBJECTIVES
To recognise the link between Rosh Hashana and Yom Kippur and understand its importance in the Jewish religion.

CURRICULUM LINKS
PSHE and citizenship: KS2 2e – to reflect on spiritual and cultural issues; 2i – to appreciate the range of religious and ethnic identities in the United Kingdom.

Yom Kippur

What you need
Drawing and painting materials; a member of the Jewish community could come into school and explain both Rosh Hashana and Yom Kippur to the children.

Background
Yom Kippur is the most solemn day in the Jewish calendar and people fast for 25 hours. They will eat a large meal before the fast begins, although children under 13 and people who are ill or pregnant do not have to fast. On the day itself many people will wear white clothes; they won't wear any make up or perfume and some Jews will not wear leather shoes. They will also not have a bath for the rest of the 25 hours so many Jewish people have a ritual bath beforehand that prepares them for the holy day. There are five services in the synagogue and at the end of the day the sound of the ram's horn (the shofar) marks the end of the celebrations. It takes place in early October and is a day to reflect on the past year and ask God's forgiveness for any sins. During the ten days between Rosh Hashana and Yom Kippur everyone takes the opportunity to put things right with other people. (Ideally children will have already looked at how Rosh Hashana is celebrated, see page 8.)

What to do
● Explain that Yom Kippur begins at sunset on the tenth day after Rosh Hashana (remind the children briefly about Rosh Hashana – page 8).
● Talk about what happens during Yom Kippur.
● Why do they think that children under 13 and people who are pregnant or ill do not have to fast?
● Ask the children what 'bad' things they have done during the past year. What have they done to put them right?
● Discuss how to make a poster that will tell everyone not to do the 'bad' things but to do only 'good' things during the coming year.

Differentiation
Some children will need help with designing a poster – even with choosing a theme. Very able children could be asked to make lists of the 'bad' things chosen by the class and create a large 'We are not going to behave like this again' display sheet for other children to look at.

AGE RANGE 7–9

LEARNING OBJECTIVES
To understand why Sukkot is celebrated and to use technology skills to create a 'Sukkah'.

CURRICULUM LINKS
Religious education: QCA Unit 1D 'Beliefs and practice' – to understand that festivals are celebrations of symbolic significance for believers.
Design and technology: KS2 1b – to develop ideas and explain them clearly; 2d – to assemble and join components accurately.

Sukkot

What you need
Shoe boxes; coloured paper and card; scissors, paints, glue and threads; leaves and straw; copies of 'Sukkah design' photocopiable page 26.

Background
Sukkot is the harvest festival commemorating the time when the Jewish people wandered in the desert after the exodus from Egypt. It lasts for a week and, in warm countries, a hut or Sukkah is built in their garden and they eat and sleep there. There is a special service in the synagogue where people hold branches of palms and willow trees and carry a yellow fruit like a lemon. Jews also give money to the homeless and Sukkot is a time to welcome visitors and feed them.

What to do
● Ask the children what they think the word 'harvest' means. Use the answers for discussion. Write useful information on the whiteboard. (Develop ideas such as crops, fruit, vegetables, farmers, the foods that we eat and how some countries have very poor harvests.)
● Suggest the link between Sukkot as a harvest festival and the school's own harvest festival.
● Explain the story of the 40-year period when the Jewish people were wandering in the desert.
● Ask the children what they know about deserts and what grows there, and explain the details of how Sukkot is celebrated.
● Explain that they are going to use their shoe boxes to make their own Sukkah.
● Remind them that the Sukkah is for eating and sleeping in. It has a partially open roof so that the sky can be seen and the roof is covered with branches and hung with the harvest of fruit and vegetables.
● Give them photocopiable page 26.
● Make sure that the children discuss what they are trying to design with other children. They need to know what they are going to use, how they are going to fasten or stick it and what material it is made of.
● Make the Sukkahs and display them alongside the story of Sukkot.

Differentiation
Allow less able children more time to discuss how they will make their sukkah and support them more as they write or draw their designs.

AGE RANGE 9–11

LEARNING OBJECTIVES
To understand the significance of the Battle of Trafalgar and to understand why Lord Nelson is thought to be an important hero.

CURRICULUM LINKS
History: KS2 1a – to place events and people into correct periods of time; 4a – to find out about events and people from an appropriate range of sources.
NLS: Y6 T1 Text 15 – to develop a journalistic style.

Trafalgar Day

What you need
Pictures of ships and of Nelson; maps to show where the Battle of Trafalgar took place; newspaper and magazine articles about modern-day heroes; writing equipment and painting/drawing materials.

Background
Admiral Lord Horatio Nelson is one of the best remembered heroes in British history. He was born on 29 September 1758 in Norfolk. His father was the vicar. Nelson joined the Royal Navy at the age of 12 and eventually became a captain. He led his men in boarding parties onto enemy ships and because of his reckless bravery he lost an eye and part of his right arm had to be amputated – without anaesthetic. Nelson

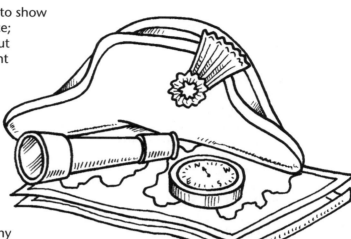

was a great leader and his men thought that he looked after them well. At the Battle of Trafalgar he led a fleet of 27 ships straight at the French, which split the French fleet in half and allowed the British ships to move around and defeat them. Nelson stood on the deck of the *Victory* in his colourful uniform to inspire his men but was shot by a sniper. He died, knowing that he had won, a few hours later. His body was taken back to England, preserved in a barrel of brandy, and he was buried in St Paul's Cathedral. Trafalgar Day celebrates his victory over the French and Spanish fleets on 21 October 1805. By defeating both the French and Spanish, Nelson prevented them combining together and invading Britain.

What to do
● Make sure that the children take notes. At the same time, write key words on the whiteboard or OHP.
● Ask the children who their heroes are – expect footballers, soap opera stars and singers.
● Discuss how, 200 years ago, Nelson was the equivalent of these heroes and was already popular even before the Battle of Trafalgar.
● Ask who has heard of Nelson and find out what they already know.
● Give the children the basic facts about Nelson.
● Tell the children that they are going to use their notes and any other information, including pictures, to illustrate and write a newspaper article about Nelson the hero and the Battle of Trafalgar.
● Look together at some articles about current heroes in newspapers and magazines and tell the children that they will have time to do further research on the internet and in the library.
● Remind the children to think about the kinds of information they will want to use to make Nelson sound like a hero.

Differentiation
Less able children may need writing frames and support in note taking and writing.
More able children could do different kinds of writing, such as an obituary of Nelson.

United Nations Day

AGE RANGE 9–11

LEARNING OBJECTIVES
To understand more about the United Nations and how it affects children.

CURRICULUM LINKS
Citizenship: QCA Unit 7 'Children's rights – human rights' – to understand the difference between wants, needs and rights.

What you need
Art materials for a poster; Article 31 of the UN Convention on the Rights of the Child written on the whiteboard.

Background
United Nations Day is celebrated on 24 October. The organisation was formed in 1945 to draw up a charter of peace after the Second World War and to prevent another global war. The United Nations has 191 member countries (almost every country in the world) and it has its own headquarters in New York with its own flag, post office and stamps. The main purpose of the UN is to – *preserve peace, advance justice and remove poverty, disease and illiteracy in the world, to stop environmental destruction and to encourage respect for each other's rights and freedoms.*

What to do
● Discuss with the children the objectives of the UN and what it stands for. One of their main purposes is the welfare of children all over the world.
● Ask them what problems children in other countries might have – encourage the children to think about poverty, lack of food and water, bad housing, violence, no education and so on. List them on the whiteboard.
● Read the children Article 31 of the United Nations Convention on the Rights of the Child. It says:
    1.   Every child has the right to rest and leisure, to engage in play and recreational activities appropriate to the age of the child and to participate freely in cultural life and the arts.
    2.   Member governments shall respect and promote the right of the child to participate fully in cultural and artistic life and shall encourage the provision of appropriate and equal opportunities for cultural, artistic, recreational and leisure activities.
● Discuss what this means. Ask the children to create a poster that shows important things such as 'rest', 'leisure' and 'play' which are essential for children all over the world.
● Display the posters alongside a copy of Article 31.

Differentiation
Less able children will need help with the concepts and their poster could be limited to the 'right to play'. More able children could use the internet to find more UN Articles that apply to children and schools.

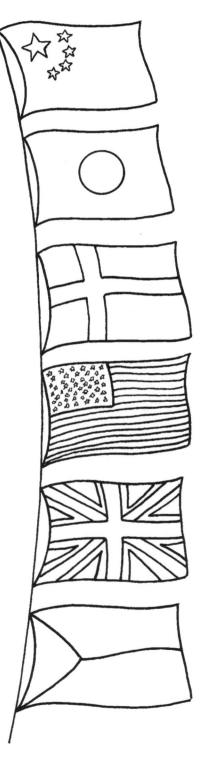

Festivals

AGE RANGE 7–11

LEARNING OBJECTIVES
To understand more about the customs and traditions of Halloween.

CURRICULUM LINKS
English: KS2 Drama 4b – to use character, action and narrative to convey a story in a play that is devised and scripted by the children.
Art and design: QCA Unit 6B 'What a performance' – to investigate headwear and costume in different cultures.

Halloween

What you need
Card to make masks and templates of two or three animal masks; yellow or orange paper for pumpkin lanterns; string, wool and paints; copies of traditional stories and fables; small tealights.

Background
Halloween, on 31 October, is a very old celebration. It started when the Celts celebrated their new year with a festival called Samhain that marked the end of the season of the Sun – summer. The Celts thought that evil spirits came in the darkness and that the spirits of the dead would take on the form of animals. They would dress up in masks and animal skins, carry lanterns and light bonfires to keep the spirits away. Other Halloween traditions, many of which are more recent, include making pumpkin lanterns, apple bobbing (which is probably Roman), dressing up to avoid being recognised and 'trick or treat'. Nuts and apples were also used to tell fortunes and Halloween was sometimes known as Nutcrack Night or Snap Apple Night, when families would sit round fires telling stories.

What to do
● Discuss with the children the background to Halloween and the different ways of celebrating it. It is important to talk about the problems that can be caused by trick and treating, especially with older people, and the dangers of going out on their own.
● Make animal masks using card. Use stronger card to make templates of two or three different animals. The children can then use the templates to make their own and decorate them using wool, string and paints.
● Use yellow or orange paper to make 2D pumpkin lanterns. Make these as fierce as possible. It will help to draw some shapes of eyes and mouths on the whiteboard.
● Read the children four or five traditional stories, such as fables or fairy stories.
● Ask them to work in groups of approximately six and give each group a copy of one of the stories.
● Each group should work out how to tell their story to rest of the class.
● Towards the end of the afternoon, light the small tealights (taking into account all health and safety regulations) and sit together, wearing the masks and telling the prepared stories.

Differentiation
More able children will be able to develop their stories in more complex ways.

AGE RANGE 7–9

LEARNING OBJECTIVES
To begin to understand the concept of 'saints' and what All Saints Day actually celebrates.

CURRICULUM LINKS
Religious education: KS2 2e – to reflect on sources of inspiration in their own and others' lives.
NLS: Y3–4 Vocabulary extension – to collect new words and create ways of categorising and logging them.

All Saints Day

What you need
Sheets of paper approximately 5 × 15cm; templates for leaves; large display paper and display board; drawing materials and paints.

Background
The first day of November is known as All Saints Day and it is when Christians honour all the saints who do not have their own special days. It used to be known as All Hallows or Hallowmas ('hallow' is an old word meaning holy person or saint). It is closely linked to the Celtic festival of Samhain and Christians adapted the festival to celebrate good conquering evil and Jesus defeating darkness.

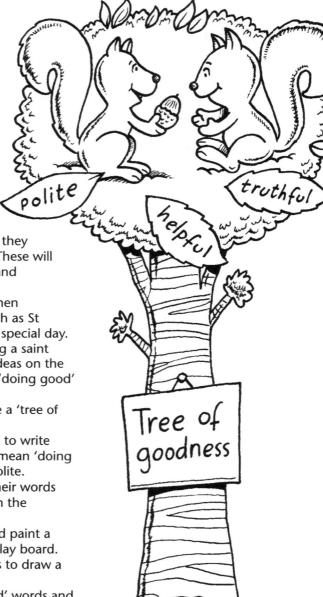

What to do
● Ask the children to list any saints that they know who have their own special days. These will include St Andrew, St David, St George and St Patrick.
● Remind them that All Saints Day is when we celebrate the lives of other saints, such as St Christopher, who do not have their own special day.
● Ask the children what they think being a saint actually means and write some of their ideas on the whiteboard. The idea of 'goodness' and 'doing good' needs to be emphasised.
● Tell them that they are going to make a 'tree of goodness'.
● First of all ask each child on their own to write down three 'good' words or words that mean 'doing good' – such as helpful, kind, truthful, polite.
● Ask the children in turn to read out their words and write them as a definitive class list on the whiteboard.
● In the meantime some children should paint a large tree without any leaves for the display board.
● Using the templates, each child needs to draw a leaf and colour it.
● They need to choose one of the 'good' words and write it on their leaf.
● The leaves can all be stuck on to the 'tree of goodness'.

Differentiation
The less able children will need help with the 'good' words and if they are having problems need only find one; the more able could find all the saints. But all children will be capable of helping to make leaves and writing the words on to them.

AGE RANGE 9–11

LEARNING OBJECTIVES
To understand the significance and some of the traditional ways of celebrating All Souls Day and what it means to Christians.

CURRICULUM LINKS
Religious education: KS2 3h – to learn about the journey of life and death, and what people think about life after death.

All Souls Day

What you need
Copies of 'All Souls cakes' photocopiable page 27; ingredients for the cakes; a toy hobby horse – or picture of one.

Background
All Souls Day, on 2 November, gives Christians the opportunity to remember and pray for people who have died. Like Halloween and All Saints Day, it has its origins in a Celtic festival when candles and bonfires were lit to light the souls' way to their life after death. All Souls night was the time when the dead were able to revisit their homes and meals and wine were left out for refreshment. Poor people would offer prayers to the dead for rich people. In return they recieved food or money for food. It was a bit like carol singing at Christmas. Poor people would go 'souling' and in some villages one of the 'soulers' would have a hobby horse. People would give the 'soulers' 'soul' cakes.

What to do
● Give the children the background to All Souls Day and ask them which other festivals around this time have light as one of their key themes. Make sure that Divali, All Saints Day and Eid are discussed.
● Discuss with them how light symbolises goodness and darkness – evil. Explain that in many faiths light is used to show how good triumphs over bad.
● Check with parents and carers for any food allergies or dietary requirements, then help the children make their own soul cakes. As many adults as possible will be needed to help the children, especially in separating the eggs. (Take care when using a hot oven.)

Differentiation
Less able children will need help in reading the recipe and could work in pairs. More able children could find All Souls Day prayers.

AGE RANGE 5–9

LEARNING OBJECTIVES
To understand some of the main elements of Divali and how the festival is celebrated.

CURRICULUM LINKS
Religious education: QCA Unit 1D 'Beliefs and practice' – to understand that festivals are celebrations of symbolic significance for believers; Unit 3B 'How and why do Hindus celebrate Divali?' – to know why Divali is important to Hindus and to give an account of the story of Rama and Sita.

Divali

What you need
Clay; tealights; copies of 'Making divas' photocopiable page 28; craft materials to make simple stick puppets; pictures of Rama, Sita, Lakshmana, Hanuman and Ravana; a story of Rama and Sita – view the online picture gallery of Hindu gods at www.hindunet.com.au; samosas and Indian sweets.

Background
Divali is celebrated by Hindus worldwide. It lasts for five days in late October or early November and is a joyful festival of lights in honour of Lakshmi, the Hindu goddess of wealth and prosperity, and celebrates the return of Rama and Sita. Prince Rama and his wife Sita were banished for 14 years from their home in the city of Ayodhya by her father, the king, and sent into the forest with Rama's brother Lakshmana. Sita was then kidnapped by a ten-headed demon called Ravana and taken to the island of Lanka. Rama got help from the monkey warrior Hanuman and rescued his wife. They escaped from the forest and returned to Ayodhya by following rows of lights to guide them. Rama was crowned king. Divali means 'rows of lighted lamps' and lamps are placed around the home and in the street. The more lamps there are the more likely that the goddess Lakshmi will bring wealth and prosperity. During the festival people dress up in their best clothes, meet their friends and family, eat special food and give each other sweets.

What to do
● Tell the children the background to Divali and how, in the story of Rama and Sita, good wins over evil.
● Write key words and names on the whiteboard, and ask the children to write their own version of the story.
● Look at illustrations of the characters, and ask the children to produce simple stick puppets to illustrate their version.
● Using the 'Making divas' photocopiable sheet on page 28, make divas or clay light holders. When they are dry put a tealight in each one.
● At the end of the day, light all the tealights (following all health and safety guidelines). Use the stick puppets to dramatise the story of Rama and Sita and enjoy eating the samosas and sweets.

Differentiation
Less able children may need a writing framework and help with the story. More able children can be provided with a fuller version and expected to produce more detailed writing.

AGE RANGE 7–9

LEARNING OBJECTIVES
To understand more about the festival of Ramadan and the discipline that it requires.

CURRICULUM LINKS
Religious education: KS2 3e – to understand how people's beliefs impact on their lives; 3k – to understand what is expected of a person in following a religion or belief.
Science: QCA Unit 5A 'Keeping healthy' – to identify the components of a healthy and balanced diet, especially if a person is fasting during the day.

Ramadan

What you need
Paints or pastels, crayons and paper; writing paper; paintings of sunsets by famous artists.

Background
Ramadan takes place in late October and early November, in the ninth month of the Islamic calendar, and is when Muslims across the world will fast during the hours of daylight. They believe that it is the time when the gates of heaven are open and the gates of hell are closed; a time to strengthen family and community links. People will eat a light meal before dawn and eat after the sun has set. Many who are too old, sick or have children who are too young to fast, will give money to charity on each day when they eat during Ramadan.

What to do
● Discuss with the children some of the facts about Ramadan. Make sure that they understand that every Muslim is expected to fast from sunrise to sunset and that this is very difficult.
● Emphasise that fasting each day takes a lot of discipline. Make a list of things they do that require discipline and commitment – such as different sports, learning a musical instrument and lessons in school.
● Ask the children to write each of the things that they do that require discipline on a sheet of paper. Underneath each heading write down what happens if you do have discipline – the 'pros', and what happens if you do not have discipline – the 'cons'.
● Repeat the fact that Muslims fast from dawn to dusk for 30 days. They must look forward to sunset so that they can eat. Show the children different pictures of sunsets.
● Paint pictures of sunsets and display them so that there is space for each child to write down what they would like to eat after a long day of fasting.
● Each child could also write a sentence stating what they are going to do that requires commitment and discipline, for example, 'I am going to practise my guitar every day' or 'I am going to do at least one job to help at home every week'.

Differentiation
More able children can write in more detail about Ramadan, including praying five times a day and the five pillars of Islam. Less able children will need help with 'pros' and 'cons' and with words for what they want to eat.

AGE RANGE 5–11

LEARNING OBJECTIVES
To understand more about the customs and festival of Eid and how it is linked to the end of Ramadan.

CURRICULUM LINKS
Religious education: QCA Unit 1D 'Beliefs and practice' – to understand that festivals are celebrations of symbolic significance for believers.
Art and design: QCA Unit 3B 'Investigating pattern' – to investigate patterns in textiles in different cultures (such as Islamic prayer mats).

Eid-ul-Fitr

What you need
White and coloured card; pencils, crayons, scissors, glue, sequins and glitter; illustrations of Islamic patterns and artwork.

Background
The happy Muslim festival of Eid-ul-Fitr celebrates the end of fasting during Ramadan and begins on the first day of the new moon. It is also about thanking Allah for the help and strength they were given that helped them fast during Ramadan. During Eid, many Muslims wear their best clothes, decorate their houses and go to special services in the mosque. They make sure that they have given something to charity to help people who are poor. They also eat a special meal during the day. This will be the first daytime meal since Ramadan started. Muslims also send special cards to each other decorated with bright colours and patterns. They sometimes have the words 'Eid Mubarak' written in Arabic, which means 'have a happy and blessed Eid'.

What to do
● Ask the children what days they celebrate that are happy ones – such as birthdays, Christmas and Easter.
● Make a list on the whiteboard of what they do that makes it a happy time.
● Explain to the children that during the special time of Eid some of the things a person is expected to do will include:
    1.   having a haircut (men only)
    2.   brushing your teeth
    3.   cutting finger and toe nails
    4.   having a bath
    5.   wearing new or best clothes
    6.   wearing perfume
    7.   eating something sweet.
● Compare and discuss these with the children's list on the whiteboard – there should be some similarities. For example, most of their special occasions will also involve being clean and wearing nice clothes, and both Christmas and Easter mean eating sweet things.
● The children can make Eid cards. These can be simple 2D cards or be as technologically complex as you want. They could, for example, have moving parts or have an inside that has a 'pop up' structure. Another way to make the cards is to use some of the Islamic patterns as decoration.

Differentiation
Less able children may need help with describing their own celebrations and with any complex card designs. More able children can write their own account of the meaning of Eid-ul-Fitr and make cards that show a high standard of technology.

Guy Fawkes/ Bonfire Night

AGE RANGE 5–11

LEARNING OBJECTIVE
To recognise the reason for celebrating the Gunpowder Plot.

CURRICULUM LINKS
History: Adapted Unit (Year 2) 'What do we know about Guy Fawkes and the Gunpowder Plot?' – to learn how people affect events in history and in the present.
Art and design: KS1 and KS2 2b – to apply different techniques to materials and processes (in creating the bonfire and night sky background).
Design and technology: KS1 and KS2 5c – to carry out assignments using food.

What you need
Art materials, including glitter and sequins; display board; reference books with details of the Gunpowder Plot; copies of 'Gunpowder treason and plot poem' photocopiable page 29.

Background
The anniversary of the Gunpowder Plot, when Guy Fawkes tried to blow up the king and Parliament with gunpowder, is remembered on 5 November. The celebrations include burning the 'Guy' on a bonfire and letting off fireworks. In 1605 Guy Fawkes and a group of other Catholic men placed barrels of gunpowder in the cellars underneath the Houses of Parliament. They wanted to kill King James and his government because they felt that he was treating Catholics unfairly. Guy Fawkes was watching over the barrels of gunpowder ready to light the fuse. Soldiers discovered him and he was put in prison and tortured. All of the plotters were arrested and all were executed.

What to do
● Tell the children the basic story of Guy Fawkes.
● Ask them how they celebrate Bonfire Night and tell them about other traditions, such as: making a guy and 'penny for the guy', letting off fireworks (this is a good opportunity for reminding children of all the safety aspects related to fires and fireworks), eating food such as sausages, baked potatoes and parkin (a sticky ginger cake); some towns have torch-lit processions and carry flaming barrels through the streets.
● Make a big wall display by painting a background on the display board of a bonfire and night sky. Make a 3D guy using material remnants and stick this on to the bonfire.
● Children can design and make fireworks – both the tube and the sparks and flames. Use glitter and sequins to make them sparkle. Stick these onto the display as well.
● At the end of the day nearest to 5 November, turn off the lights and read the poem on the photocopiable sheet together.
● Use music to make it more atmospheric, for example Wagner's *Ride of the Valkyries* or Handel's *Fireworks* suite.

Differentiation
Some children can do research on the internet or using books and write an illustrated account of the plot as a newspaper report. There are many recipes for parkin and making this tasty treat can be enjoyable for some children to do. Some less able children may need help reading the recipe.

Remembrance Day

AGE RANGE 5–11

LEARNING OBJECTIVES
To begin to understand the importance of Remembrance Day; why poppies are worn, who we are remembering and what happens in towns, cities and villages across the country.

CURRICULUM LINKS
History: QCA Unit 17 'What are we remembering on Remembrance Day?' – to investigate the origins of Remembrance Day; KS2 2c – to identify and describes reasons for, and results of, historical events.

What you need

Writing and drawing materials; poppies; books about the First World War; copies of 'For the Fallen' photocopiable page 30.

Background

At 11.00am on 11 November 1918 (the eleventh hour of the eleventh day of the eleventh month), the fighting stopped in the First World War. Remembrance Day commemorates all those who were killed in that war, in the Second World War and all other wars. Services of remembrance are held on the Sunday nearest to 11 November. Members of the royal family and government attend the service in London and go to the Cenotaph. On 11 November there is a two minute silence at 11 o'clock.

What to do

● Ask the children why we wear poppies. Explain that on the battlefields of France they were the first flowers to grow in the churned up earth.
● Arrange a visit to the local war memorial to draw what they see.
● Children (especially from small towns and villages) may have the names of relations on the war memorial. Their stories can answer the question – Who do we remember?
● Using the photocopiable sheet, read and talk about the extract of Laurence Binyon's poem 'For the Fallen' (the extract is the third and fourth stanzas). It is important to stress that they were very young men who died and they did not get the chance to grow old like everyone else. This is why it is important for us to remember them.
● Ask the children who they remember – suggest pets, grandparents, or other friends who have moved away. Handle this sensitively as some children may have had a recent bereavement of some kind in the family
● Ask why it is important to remember people and what happens if we do not.
● Explain that we all live busy lives and often don't get the opportunity to think quietly. This is why there is two minutes' silence on Remembrance Day.
● Hold a two minute silence. Ask the children to think about their feelings and what they see, hear and feel during it, and to write about it afterwards.

Differentiation

More able children can do further research and find out about other First World War poets. Less able children will need help and support with the writing and can be limited to just a sentence. They could also be encouraged to draw pictures and illustrations.

AGE RANGE 7–11

LESSON OBJECTIVES
To recognise why Guru Nanak is such an important
figure in the Sikh religion and to begin to understand
some of his teachings.

CURRICULUM LINKS
Religious education: KS2 3j – to learn about figures
from whom believers find inspiration.

Guru Nanak's Birthday

What you need
Paper; gold and silver pens, paints, pastels, glitter and sequins; books about the Sikh religion.

Background
Guru Nanak, born in 1469, is the founder of the Sikh religion which is still based on his teachings. At the age of 30 Guru Nanak went swimming in a river and disappeared. Everyone thought he had drowned but three days later he reappeared. He said that when he had been in the river he had seen a vision of God who had given him messages for everyone. He began to preach the Sikh faith and spent the rest of his life travelling round the world. The birthday of Guru Nanak is celebrated in early November. A reading of the whole of the Sikh Holy Scriptures (Guru Granth Sahib) begins 48 hours before the day of his birthday and is completed by teams of men and women. The Gurdwaras where Sikhs pray are decorated with flowers and there are prayers and singing. The day usually ends with a feast.

What to do
● Ask the children what they already know about Guru Nanak, then tell them the story about him.
● Discuss each of the messages below from his teachings. Make sure that the children think about what each one means to them. Make a list of the key points they make.
  1. work hard and help others
  2. be honest
  3. everyone is equal – rich and poor, male and female, black and white
  4. be kind to all birds, animals and people
  5. always speak the truth.
● Each child should choose one of the five teachings.
● Fold a piece of cartridge paper in half and ask the children to write their chosen message on the front and decorate it with some images from books about Sikhism.
● The message could be written in bright colours or with a gold or silver pen.
● The children should draw a picture of what the message means to them inside the folded paper. This picture should be bright and colourful with lots of sequins and glitter.
● Display the pictures by hanging them on strings across the classroom.

Differentiation
More able children could find out more about Guru Nanak and write and illustrate the story of his life. Less able children should be able to do all the activities with support.

AGE RANGE 7–11

LEARNING OBJECTIVES
To understand why the Pilgrims went to America and to recognise why 'Thanksgiving' is such an important celebration for Americans.

CURRICULUM LINKS
History: KS2 1a – to place events into correct periods of time; 2c – to identify and describes reasons for, and results of, historical events.

Thanksgiving

What you need
World map and map of America; pictures of the *Mayflower* and period costumes (see www.mayflowerhistory.com or http://teacher.scholastic.com/thanksgiving/mayflower/tour/index.htm); squares of card to go on display board; examples of menus; paper and art materials.

Background
The American Thanksgiving, on the fourth Thursday in November, celebrates a year of survival for the first European settlers to America. In September 1620, more than 100 Pilgrims set sail from Plymouth across the Atlantic to settle in what was known as the New World. They were families with children who wanted to live a simpler life according to their own religious beliefs. After a journey of 66 days they arrived at Cape Cod, Massachusetts. They named the place Plymouth Harbour. Their first winter was difficult and half the colony died. In the spring the Native Americans taught them how to grow maize (corn) and where to hunt and fish. The following autumn many of the original colonists celebrated the harvest with a feast of thanks.

What to do
● Tell the story of the settlers in America and the first Thanksgiving.
● Look on a map of America to see where the Pilgrim Fathers landed and at some of the 'English' place names which can be found there.
● Find out about some of the food that the Pilgrims found, such as corn, wild turkeys and cranberries.
● Ask the children what they have to be thankful for. Get as many ideas as possible and write them on individual squares of card. These can be used to make a Thanksgiving board.
● Tell the children that they are going to write and design a menu for their own 'Thanksgiving' meal. Show them what a menu looks like – with starters, main courses and dessert. Discuss some ideas for their favourite meals before they start.
● Decorate the borders of the menu with Thanksgiving symbols such as turkeys, corn and berries.

Differentiation
More able children could do further research about the early settlers and write this up with illustrations to go alongside the Thanksgiving board. Some children might like to learn more about cranberries because they were used not only as a food but also as a medicine and dye. Less able children will need help with their ideas for menus.

AGE RANGE 5–11

LEARNING OBJECTIVES
To understand and learn more about what Advent means to Christians and to make an Advent calendar.

CURRICULUM LINKS
Religious education: KS1 1b – to explore celebrations in religion; 1d – to explore how religious beliefs and ideas can be expressed through the arts; KS2 1a – to describe the key aspects of religions; 3i – to understand how religious ideas are expressed in symbols.

Advent

What you need
Thin card or stiff paper for each child; old Christmas cards, glue, sequins and art materials; pencils and felt-tipped pens; copies of 'Making an Advent calendar' photocopiable page 31.

Background
Advent begins on the Sunday nearest to 30 November and is the start of the Christmas season. During this period Christians prepare for the birth of Jesus by planning what gifts they will buy, singing carols, decorating their houses with holly, Christmas trees and Advent wreaths made of evergreen leaves, twigs and branches.

What to do
● Explain what Advent means to Christians and how important the weeks leading up to the festival of Christmas are.
● Ask the children what preparations their families make for Christmas.
● Explain that they are going to make an Advent calendar.
● Photocopiable page 31 shows the basic design. As the season of Advent begins at the end of November, the calendar usually has 24 equal spaces for the days of December, with a larger one for Christmas day.
● Each child will need a piece of stiff paper or thin card. Mark it with 24 small squares and one larger one.
● Ask the children what they can draw and decorate behind each of the doors. Each one of the 25 squares must be decorated with something linked to Christmas.
● They will need 25 squares that fit over each of the drawings. Stick each one down on one edge so that they will open like doors to show the drawing underneath. (These can be standardised sizes and pre-cut.)
● Check that each of the doors opens and decorate the front of the calendar and each of the doors as brightly as possible. Number each of the doors.

Differentiation
This is a difficult task and all children will need some help. Check that they can glue the doors down properly. If it is too difficult you could make a class one on a display board with 25 of the children's illustrations covered up and ready to be opened on the correct day.

St Andrew's Day

AGE RANGE 5–11

LEARNING OBJECTIVES
To recognise the importance of St Andrew as the patron saint of Scotland and to understand the legends about his life.

CURRICULUM LINKS
History: KS1 2a – to recognise why people did things, why events happened and what happened as a result; KS2 2b – to learn about the social, cultural, religious and ethnic diversity of the societies studied in Britain.

What you need
Large paper to make a class book; paper and equipment for drawings and illustrations.

Background
St Andrew is the patron saint of Scotland and his life is celebrated on 30 November. He was one of Jesus' 12 disciples and the brother of St Peter. He was crucified on a diagonal cross, which is why the Scottish flag is a white diagonal cross on a blue background.

What to do
● Explain to the class that they are going to illustrate a book about St Andrew.
● Tell the children some of these legends and stories about St Andrew:
1. he was crucified on a diagonal cross
2. his bones (tooth, arm, kneecap and fingers) were brought back from Greece by boat to Scotland
3. Angus, the Scottish King who was given the bones, had a dream before a battle that he would win and a white cross appeared in the sky
4. St Rule brought the bones of St Andrew to Scotland and founded the town of St Andrews. A cathedral was built and the ruins can still be seen today
5. St Andrew's Day used to be a popular feast day. One of the customs was to go St Andrews to catch rabbits and hares to eat
6. girls who wanted to get married would throw a shoe at a door on St Andrew's day. If the shoe pointed to the way out it meant that she would leave the house and marry within the year.

● St Andrew's Day is also linked to the time of the year when human beings could turn into vampires. To avoid this people placed garlic on their windows and rubbed it on their cattle.
● Each of the stories will need illustrating together with a simplified written explanation.

Differentiation
Less able children will need help in choosing what to illustrate and will need help in deciding what to draw/paint. More able children could produce illustrations as comic strips or as part of newspaper reports or television documentaries, for example, *Saint's bones arrive by ship* or *St Andrews woman finds husband!*

Harvest scones

- Have as many adults working with the children as possible and beware of hot ovens and bun trays.

Ingredients [makes about 8–12]
225g self raising flour
110g caster sugar
110g butter, margarine or other appropriate spread
Handful of raisins
Enough milk to make a sticky but not too runny dough

Equipment
You will need a bun tray, mixing basin, mixing spoon, table spoon and scales.

- Set the oven temperature to 180°C.
- Mix together the flour and sugar with hands or spoon.
- Rub the butter into the flour mixture until it looks like breadcrumbs.
- Mix in a handful of raisins and add a little milk.
- Stir with the mixing spoon to make a sticky dough. Add a little more milk if necessary.
- Grease the bun tray with a little butter or margarine.
- Place approximately a tablespoon of the mixture in each section of the tray.
- Place the tray in the oven for about 15 minutes.
- When they are ready they will be brown on top and have risen slightly.
- Remove from the oven and as soon as they are cool enough to handle take the scones out of the tray and leave them to cool.
- They can be eaten with jam – which is another example of fruits and harvest.

Sukkah design

● Complete this sheet – discuss it with your partner or other children and with a teacher or classroom assistant before you start making the model.

● Draw the box with its walls coloured and designed and its roof covered with leaves and fruits.

● List some of the materials you will use for the roof and how it will be stuck together.

_____

_____

_____

● Draw some of the furniture that you will put in the Sukkah. Remember not to make them too big or too small.

● What material will you use and how will you stick it together?

_____

_____

All Souls cakes

Ingredients
175g soft butter/margarine or other spread
175g sugar
3 egg yolks
450g plain flour
Teaspoon of cinnamon, mace or all spice

Equipment
You will need scales, a wooden spoon, a large mixing bowl, saucer, eggcup, 5cm round pastry cutter, bun tray, baking paper (optional), cooling rack and oven gloves.

• Set the oven to 180°C.

• Cream the butter and sugar together.

• Ask an adult to help you to separate the eggs. Break the egg on to a saucer and then carefully place an eggcup over the yolk. Hold the eggcup in place while you tip away the egg white.

• Beat in the egg yolks.

• Sift in the flour and spices and mix to a dough.

• Roll out to 1cm thick and cut into 5cm rounds.

• Put on greased bun trays or baking paper.

• Bake the cakes for approximately 20–25 minutes. Check them regularly after 15 minutes.

• When slightly cooled place on a wire rack to cool.

Making divas

You will need a piece of clay about the size of a small apple and a tealight.

• Roll the clay into a ball.	
• Hold the ball of clay in the palm of your hand and push the thumb of the other hand into the ball but not through it.	
• Squeeze the ball between thumb and fingers and move the ball around so the hole is an even shape.	
• Flatten the base of the lamp by putting it on newspaper and pull out the front and back to make the shape of the lamp. Leave to dry.	

Gunpowder treason and plot poem

Remember, remember the fifth of November,
gunpowder, treason and plot,
I see no reason why gunpowder treason
should ever be forgot.

Guy Fawkes, Guy Fawkes,
'twas his intent
to blow up the King and the Parliament.
Three score barrels of powder below,
Poor old England to overthrow:
By God's providence he was catched
With a dark lantern and burning match.

'For the Fallen'

by Laurence Binyon

They went with songs to the battle, they were young,
Straight of limb, true of eye, steady and aglow.
They were staunch to the end against odds uncountered;
They fell with their faces to the foe.

They shall grow not old, as we that are left grow old;
Age shall not weary them, nor the years contemn.
At the going down of the sun and in the morning
We will remember them.

(Stanzas three and four)

Making an Advent calendar

● Each child should draw 25 small Christmas pictures on their piece of card in the marked squares.

● Give each child the right number of small rectangles to cover each of the decorated squares on their card. Stick each one down to make a door over the picture.

● Repeat for each of the squares and number each one, from 1 to 25 – colour the numbers in bright colours and decorate the doors and the front of the calendar.

CHAPTER 2

Winter
December to February

AGE RANGE 5–7

LEARNING OBJECTIVES
To help children understand the legend of
St Nicholas, how the festival is celebrated in
different countries and the similarities between
St Nicholas and Santa Claus (Father Christmas).

CURRICULUM LINKS
PSHE and citizenship: KS1 1a – to recognise
what is right and wrong; 4a – to recognise how
their behaviour affects other people; 4d – that
family and friends should care for each other.

St Nicholas

What you need
Pictures and information about St Nicholas www.stnicholascenter.org; art and drawing
materials to make posters.

Background
St Nicholas' Day is celebrated on 6 December. Nicholas was the bishop of Myra in
Turkey and there are several legends and stories about him. For example, there was a
poor man who could no longer take care of his daughters or buy them food or clothes.
St Nicholas heard about his problem and decided to leave some money secretly for the
three girls. He didn't want to be seen so he climbed on to the low roof of the house
and dropped the money down the chimney. The coins landed in the girls' stockings
that they had left by the fire to dry. In Holland, *Sinterklaas* (Santa Claus) with a red
coat and white beard, along with his helper *Zwarte Piet* (Black Pete), gives gifts to good
children. On the night of 6 December he knocks on the door and presents will be left
on the doorstep or in shoes that are placed in the fireplace. In France, St Nicholas is
called *Père Noël* and he leaves presents – but only for good children. This is the same as
in Germany, where he also used to be known as 'Shaggy Goat' and travelled around the
countryside dressed in animal skins with his sack of presents to give to good children.

What to do
● Ask the children what they know about St Nicholas.
● Discuss the stories about St Nicholas with them and
emphasise that although they come from different
European countries there are several similarities. For
example – he only leaves gifts for good children.
● Let the children talk about how good they
have been and what gifts they would like from St
Nicholas.
● Design a poster in two halves – 'what I have
done to be good' and 'the gift I would like'.
● Encourage the children to think about what
it means to be good. Discuss examples of
good behaviour as well as examples of being
good to others.
● These posters could be part of the class
wall displays in the weeks leading up to
Christmas.

Differentiation
More able children could write about the
legends of St Nicholas as well as illustrating them
and making their posters.

BRIGHT IDEAS

AGE RANGE 7–11

LEARNING OBJECTIVES
To begin to understand more about the Universal Declaration of Human Rights and the reasons why Human Rights Day is celebrated.

CURRICULUM LINKS
Citizenship: QCA Unit 7 'Children's rights – human rights' – to understand that rights come with responsibilities; to recognise what is fair and unfair and the difference between right and wrong; Unit 2 'Choices' – to consider the influence of adverts and logos as a tool for persuasion.

Human Rights Day

What you need
Copies of 'A summary of some of the Universal Declaration of Human Rights' photocopiable page 47; paper and other materials to create a logo; examples of different logos.

Background
Human Rights Day is on 10 December and it celebrates the Universal Declaration of Human Rights by the United Nations in 1948. The underlying concept of the Declaration is 'fairness' and how people should be able to live together. It states that everybody has the right to life, liberty, freedom of thought, conscience and religion, to work, to be educated and to take part in government. It is one of the most important declarations in the world and should be respected by everyone.

What to do
● Using the photocopiable sheet, explain to the children what the Universal Declaration of Human Rights says. Relate each one to their lives and what it means to them and to living in this country. For example, adults vote for local councillors and for the MPs that they want. Laws are there to protect everyone by stopping people stealing and hurting other people.
● Discuss with the children what they think being 'fair' means and what they do that makes them 'fair' people.
● Write the list on the whiteboard. Their responses should be related to how they are treated by others, such as with respect, kindness, everyone treated the same and not having favourites.
● Talk to them about what they see as 'unfair', such as not being believed, being blamed for something they haven't done, not being allowed to do something that others are allowed to do, and make a similar list.
● Discuss logos and the instant impact that they are supposed to have.
● Show the children some examples of easily recognisable logos. This can be done as a quiz with lots of examples that they can try to identify.
● Ask the children to create a logo to promote Human Rights Day.

Differentiation
More able pupils could choose several of the points on the summary on the photocopiable sheet and write descriptions of and illustrate how these affect them and other children in this country. Less able children will need lots of support to understand the difficult concepts.

AGE RANGE 5–11

LEARNING OBJECTIVES
To understand some of the links between ancient festivals such as the Winter Solstice and how we celebrate Christmas.

CURRICULUM LINKS
Design and technology: KS1 and KS2 1b – to develop ideas and explain them clearly; 2d – to assemble and join components accurately.

The Winter Solstice

What you need
All the art and craft materials to make a Yule log or real logs; pictures of commercial Yule logs.

Background
The Winter Solstice, also called Yule is held on 21 or 22 December, the shortest day of the year. Holly was traditionally made into a wreath and hung on doors to tell people that this was a house that celebrated the birth of Christ. The Vikings thought that the Sun was a wheel that changed the seasons and Yule probably comes from their word *'houl'* – for wheel. Druids would cut mistletoe as a symbol of life and they thought that the Sun stood still for 12 days so they lit a huge log in the fireplace to overcome the darkness, get rid of evil spirits and bring good luck.

What to do
● Ask the children how they decorate their houses for Christmas and discuss the background to the Winter Solstice or Yule.
● To make a Yule log you will have to decide whether you will make the log or use a small real log, and whether you will use real greenery or make it out of paper and tissue.
● First of all, look at some pictures of Yule logs. Ask the children to design their own Yule logs.
● If you are making a log it will mean you have to make a cylinder before painting it.
● The made or real log should have appropriate greenery (such as pine leaves, cones and holly) stuck on it, or leaves made from paper and tissue. Snow can be made from cotton wool or sprays can be used. (These must only be used by an adult outside the classroom.) It is important not to use mistletoe, as the berries are poisonous. Holly and yew berries, bark and leaves are also poisonous.
● The Yule log needs to represent light so small candles need to be attached to it. (Check the school's health and safety policy.)
● All the logs will make a good pre-Christmas display so it is important to start well before the actual date of the Winter Solstice.

Differentiation
Less able children will need adult help in both designing and making the log. More able children can write the history of Yule logs. This will make good background information for the display of logs.

AGE RANGE 5–11

LEARNING OBJECTIVES
To summarise why we have Christmas and to recognise some of the traditions.

CURRICULUM LINKS
Religious education: QCA Unit 1C 'Celebrations: Why do Christians give gifts at Christmas?'; Unit 4B 'Celebrations: Christmas journeys' – to learn about the story of the birth of Jesus.
Design and technology: KS1 and KS2 1b – to develop ideas and explain them clearly; 2d – to assemble and join components accurately.

Christmas Day

What you need
Shoe box, paper; art and craft materials to make a nativity scene; pictures of the nativity and the words to carols; copies of 'Designing a nativity scene' and 'Templates for the nativity scene' photocopiable pages 48 and 49.

Background
December is closely linked to Christmas for all Christians and many of the traditions and festivals build up to the 'mass of Christ' which is the celebration of the birth of Jesus on 25 December.

What to do
● Ask the children what they do on Christmas Day and ask them to make a timeline of their perfect day, starting from when they get up to when they go to bed. These can then be made into a wall display with illustrations.

● Remind the children why we celebrate Christmas. Make a timeline together of the events in the Christmas story. Tell the children that they are going to create a nativity scene. This needs to be started at the beginning of December so that they can be displayed before being taken home.

● Use the timeline to check that the children know who and what will need to be shown in the scene and where it will need to be set.

● Ask the children to make rough plans and designs of their scenes using the 'Designing a nativity scene' photocopiable page 48 before they start building it.

● Use a shoebox or similar and add to the outside to make it look like a stable.

● Build up the scene inside it using any materials available, including straw. There are templates and suggestions on the photocopiable page 49.

● It will be more effective if the figures are cut out and stand up to create a 3D effect.

Differentiation
More able children can do more writing and could retell the Christmas story in their own words with a modern setting. Less able children will need lots of help in designing and building their nativity scenes.

AGE RANGE 7–11

LEARNING OBJECTIVES
To understand more about the traditions of Boxing Day and how it is linked to all the information that is available about St Stephen.

CURRICULUM LINKS
NLS: Y4 T1 Text 10 – to plan a story identifying stages of its telling; Y5 T2 Text 11 – to write own versions of legends.

St Stephen's or Boxing Day

What you need
Writing and drawing materials; large art paper to make a 2D box on a display board.

Background
Boxing Day is 26 December and is a public holiday in many countries. It is also St Stephen's Day and he is remembered in the carol –
    'Good King Wenceslas looked out,
    On the feast of Stephen…'
There are several reasons why 26 December became known as Boxing Day. Boxes were placed at the back of churches to collect money for the poor and servants who usually worked on Christmas Day were given the next day off and would be given Christmas boxes or presents. Lords and ladies would 'box up' left over food to give to their servants. The butchers and grocers who used to make deliveries to large houses would call on Boxing Day to collect their gifts in return for good service. St Stephen is also the patron saint of horses and in many areas it is traditional to hold a hunt on Boxing Day.
    St Stephen had been captured and stoned to death. The Roman soldiers responsible were said to have found him hiding because of the noise a wren made. A long time ago, boys with blackened faces would knock on doors on St Stephen's Day and demand money which would be used to pay for a village dance. They would chant:
    The wren the wren, the king of all birds,
    On St Stephen's Day was caught in the furze
    Up with the penny and down with the pan,
    Give us a penny to bury the wren.

What to do
● Ask the children how they celebrate Boxing Day and make a list.
● Tell them about the background to Boxing Day and St Stephen's Day.
● Ask the children to work in small groups to research some of these stories and see whether they can find out any other information about St Stephen and Boxing Day. They should then choose one of the stories to illustrate, with a brief written description.
● The pictures can be mounted inside a large and colourful painted 2D box (representing Boxing Day) on a display board.

Differentiation
More able children can write about more than one tradition and could find out more about St Stephen. Less able children could write about one tradition and be responsible for painting the large boxes.

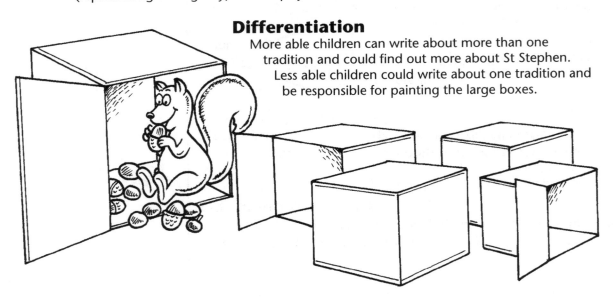

Hanukkah

AGE RANGE 5–7

LEARNING OBJECTIVES
To understand more about the Jewish festival of
Hanukkah and why it is a special time of year.

CURRICULUM LINKS
Religious education: QCA Unit 1E 'How do Jewish
people express their beliefs in practice?' – to learn
about the key features of the story of the festival of
Hanukkah and that light is used to represent the
presence of God.

What you need
Pictures of a menorah with its nine candles - called a hanukiah, see www.bracha.com;
tealights and art materials; ingredients for making pancakes (optional).

Background
Hanukkah is an eight-day Jewish festival in December, close to Christmas. It is a
Festival of Lights and celebrates a miracle in Jewish history. After a battle, the temple
in Jerusalem was destroyed. When it had been cleaned and rebuilt the menorah
(hanukaih) was lit but there was only one jar of oil. The miracle was that this lasted
eight days and the menorah with its
lights became a symbol of goodness.
Like Christmas, Hanukkah is a special
time for children, with gifts being
given on each of the eight nights.
It is also a time for eating special
foods such as latkes (potato fritters),
pancakes and doughnuts.

What to do
● Ask the children how they feel
about the dark – are they frightened?
What are they frightened of?
● Ask them how their houses are
lit. When do their parents switch the
lights on?
● Talk about light being the symbol
of goodness and tell them the story
of Hanukkah.
● Show them pictures of a nine-
stemmed menorah.
● Each child should make their own painting or drawing of a menorah – but without
any flames.
● Every day, for eight days, a flame can be drawn and coloured on their menorah.
● On the first day the centre flame and the far right-hand flame on the paper is
coloured in.
● On each subsequent day another single flame is coloured in, moving from right to
left on the picture.
● If the days are dark, tealights can be lit at this time – in the same order. (Check the
school's health and safety policy.)
● On the eighth day, with all the lights coloured on their pictures and all the tealights
lit, you can make and eat pancakes with the children (more adults will be needed to
help with this). Remind the children of the story of the oil and how the food is also
cooked in oil (as are other foods such as latkes and doughnuts).

Differentiation
More able children could write the story of the origins of Hanukkah and find and write
out a good recipe for pancakes.

New Year/ Hogmanay

AGE RANGE 5–11

LEARNING OBJECTIVES
To understand more about how New Year's Eve is celebrated and to develop ideas about new beginnings.

CURRICULUM LINKS
Citizenship: QCA Unit 2 'Choices' – to make informed choices.
PSHE and citizenship: KS1 1e – to set simple goals.

What you need
Plain paper, pencils and envelopes; a box in which to put the sealed envelopes.

Background
The start of New Year is celebrated all over the world and is a chance to look back at the old year and forward into the new one. In Scotland, Hogmanay is an important celebration. It may have come originally from the Vikings who celebrated the passing of the shortest day. Christmas was banned in Scotland for 400 years (the Scottish Presbyterian Church thought it was 'too Catholic') so it was at the New Year when friends and families got together to celebrate and exchange presents.

There are many customs associated with the New Year. The house should be cleaned on 31 December and the ashes of the fire taken out. 'Auld Lang Syne' is sung immediately after midnight. Some people go 'first footing'. This tradition says that, in order to have good luck for the rest of the year, the first person to enter the house after midnight on 31 December should be male and dark haired (perhaps having Viking blonde hair meant danger and trouble?). The man should carry coal and salt. In one part of Scotland huge fireballs are swung round on poles to represent the power of the Sun that will start to get warmer during the New Year.

What to do
● Discuss with the children how their families celebrate New Year.
● Compare the different customs with their own family celebrations.
● Discuss new beginnings, fresh starts and New Year resolutions.
● Ask them to write down one or two resolutions that they think they can keep and illustrate them.
● These should be placed in an envelope with the child's name on the front and placed in the large box.
● Open the box at the end of January and give back the resolutions to each child.
● Ask the children who kept their promise (their resolution) and who didn't.
● Discuss why it is sometimes difficult to keep promises and make new beginnings.

Differentiation
More able children can write about some of the customs and research them further. Less able children will need help to write their resolutions.

Twelfth Night (Epiphany)

AGE RANGE 5–11

LEARNING OBJECTIVES
To understand more about the Twelve Days of Christmas, what traditionally happened and the kinds of celebrations that take place.

CURRICULUM LINKS
Religious education: QCA Unit 4B: 'Celebrations: Christmas journeys' – to understand that people make special journeys to places of religious significance.
NNS: Y1–3 Counting – to know number names and recite them in order.

What you need
Art materials for a Twelfth Night freeze or timeline; the words to the song 'The Twelve Days of Christmas'.

Background
The evening of 5 January and all day 6 January is celebrated as Twelfth Night, and is the end of the Twelve Days of Christmas. For Christians, 6 January is the celebration of Epiphany, when the three kings visited the baby Jesus. Superstition says that this is also the day to take down all Christmas decorations and, if any decorations are left up, they must remain where they are until Easter Sunday. In the past many people in villages stopped working over Christmas, except for looking after the animals. The Monday after 6 January was known as Plough Monday because it was when everyone returned to work.

What to do
● Ask the children whether they know the Christmas song: 'The Twelve Days of Christmas'. If possible, sing or play it through together.
● Explain to the children what Twelfth Night and Epiphany mean, and ask them if they do anything special to celebrate it.
● Tell the children that they are going to make a 'Twelve Days of Christmas' timeline.
● The children will need to work in pairs or groups for painting and cutting out the correct number of objects for each of the 'twelve days'.
● Start the timeline well before Christmas so it is on display and waiting for when the children return to school in January. Include the dates and take down each of the correct days when the January term starts – the final one being removed on 6 January.
● You will need to make: The 'true love'; One partridge in a pear tree; Two turtledoves; Three French hens; Four calling birds; Five gold rings; Six geese a-laying; Seven swans a-swimming; Eight maids a-milking; Nine ladies dancing; Ten lords a-leaping; Eleven pipers piping and Twelve drummers drumming.

Differentiation
More able children can research the Twelve Days of Christmas, for example that each of the days is linked to Christianity: 'Ten lords a-leaping…' probably represents the ten commandments. Some children can look at numbers and try to work out exactly how many gifts 'my true love gave to me…' You will need to have the words available.

AGE RANGE 9–11

LEARNING OBJECTIVES
To recognise who Robert Burns was and to understand more about the dialect of his poems.

CURRICULUM LINKS
NLS: Y5 T2 Text 12 – to use structures of poems to write own versions; Y6 T2 Text 5 – to analyse how messages, moods, feelings and attitudes are conveyed in poetry.

Burns Night

What you need
Paper for writing; copies of 'Burns Night' photocopiable page 50; recipes for haggis – www.scottishhaggis.co.uk

Background
Robert Burns was a Scottish poet, born on 25 January 1759. He often wrote in Scottish dialect and when he died his friends started to have Burns' Suppers on 25 January to remember him. These suppers are now celebrated by Scots all over the world. Traditionally, the supper begins with a piper welcoming the guests, someone reads a grace written by Burns, the haggis – which is made of a mixture of meats, oats and spices in a sheep's stomach – is piped to the table and his poem 'To a Haggis' is read. The meal always contains haggis, mashed swede and potatoes. After it, there are more readings of his poems.

What to do
● Explain about Burns and Burns Night. Ask the children if they know any dialect and explain what dialect is.
● Give out the first half of the 'Burns Night' photocopiable sheet and read it out loud. Some children could also try reading it.
● Working in groups or pairs, ask them to write what they think these words mean: wee, sleekit, cow'rin, tim'rous, beastie.
● What animal do they think Burns is writing about? What words or phrases make them think this? What is the animal doing? What is it scared of?
● Give them the second half of the photocopiable sheet. Go through the meanings of some of the words. Tell them the title of the poem and read it again.
● In their pairs, ask them to choose an animal and write a six-line stanza. They can use free verse or the AAABAB pattern of rhymes in the Burns poem.
● Suggest that they note down some phrases about what the animal does, what it eats and where it lives, before they start.
● Read out some of the finished stanzas and then explain that they have to change some of the words into dialect – like Burns. They can make up their own words!
● When they have done this, read out some of the verses. They would make a good wall display around 25 January.

Differentiation
More able children could research dialects, such as Yorkshire, Somerset or Geordie, and write verses using those dialects. Less able children will need a lot of adult help with their writing.

AGE RANGE 9–11

LEARNING OBJECTIVES
To understand more about the Holocaust and the effect it had on a certain group of children.

CURRICULUM LINKS
History: QCA Unit 9 'What was it like for children in the Second World War?' (adapted for Year 5 and 6 children) – compare and contrast novels about children's experiences in the war.
NLS: Y6 T1 Text 11 – to distinguish between biography and autobiography.

Holocaust Memorial Day

What you need
Information about the holocaust, available for teachers from the official website: www.hmd.org.uk; copies of *The Diary of a Young Girl* by Anne Frank or books about Anne Frank; paper and writing materials.

Background
The Holocaust is a well-documented, historical event resulting in terrible atrocities. Six million people were killed by the Nazis immediately before and during the Second World War and most of those people were Jewish. On 9 and 10 November 1938 the Nazis carried out a series of brutal attacks on Jewish homes, known as the *Kristallnacht* – night of the broken glass. After this, British refugee organisations persuaded the government to allow Jewish children under 17 to come to Britain. Private individuals had to pay for their travel, their food, clothing and education. Parents were not allowed to accompany their children. Between December 1938 and the start of the War in September 1939, 10,000 Jewish children came to Britain. It was called *Kindertransport* – child transport. Most of the children never saw their parents again.

The date of 27 January has now been established as Holocaust Memorial Day, when those killed can be remembered. This is a deeply moving subject for every teacher and child and it is important to use the material available in a factual and extremely sensitive way.

What to do
● First of all tell the children as much about the Holocaust as you feel they can understand by using the official material as required.
● What do the children think the word 'refugee' means? Write down some definitions.
● Ask why people became refugees in the Second World War.
● Tell them about *Kristallnacht* and the *Kindertransport*.
● Ask the children to imagine that they are part of the *Kindertransport*. They are to write about what happened, including:
   1.   Why were they sent away?
   2.   How must their parents have felt?
   3.   How would they feel about being separated from their parents?
   4.   What would it feel like – arriving in a strange country to live with strangers?

Differentiation
Less able children will need lots of help and could illustrate the event rather than write. More able children could look at the Diary of Anne Frank and write their own five-day diary about the *Kindertransport*.

National Bird Watch

AGE RANGE 5–11

LEARNING OBJECTIVES
To understand more about common birds that visit the school to feed and to take part in a national survey of birds with the Royal Society for the Protection of Birds (RSPB).

CURRICULUM LINKS
Science: QCA Unit 2B 'Plants and animals in the local environment'; Unit 4B 'Habitats'; Unit 6A 'Interdependence and adaptation' – to recognise that there are different plants and animals in the local environment.

What you need
An area of the school where birds come to feed; different types of bird food and feeders; art paper; illustrations of common birds in books; online survey form from the RSPB website www.rspb.org.uk or telephone the RSPB and ask for a schools pack.

Background
The RSPB organises a survey of garden birds in the last few days of January. Anyone can take part in it. The survey involves watching the school garden or the area for feeding birds for an hour. You can then compare your results with others and do all kinds of research. If you prefer not to do the survey, feeding birds and trying to find the most common birds in the school garden is always an interesting thing to do.

What to do
● The whole class should do research to find out about what the most common birds are likely to be, what they eat and where they like to eat it from. The most common birds in the 2006 survey were house sparrows. But other common ones included starlings, blackbirds, blue tits and great tits, robins, greenfinches and collared doves. Less common birds that may be around in January include: field fares, song thrushes, goldfinches, dunnocks and siskins.

● The RSPB website provides all this information. There are also many books available that have high quality pictures and instructions on how to feed and identify wild birds.

● Discuss why birds need a safe place to eat and create a feeding area using different bird tables, hanging containers and a variety of foods, such as seeds, nuts and fat balls.

● If you are making a new feeding area, discuss where it should be – it should ideally be in a part of the school which is both peaceful (for the birds) and easy to observe.

● Different pairs or groups of children need to take responsibility for the area so that it stays clean and the food is regularly replaced.

● Ask the children to choose a bird to draw and colour accurately. This will mean providing high quality materials. The drawings can be part of the survey display.

Differentiation
More able children can write descriptions of the birds to mount alongside the drawings.

AGE RANGE 5–11

LEARNING OBJECTIVES
To learn more about the Chinese New Year and its customs.

CURRICULUM LINKS
Design and technology: KS1 and KS2 5c – to carry out assignments using food.
Citizenship: QCA Unit 5 'Living In a diverse world' – to appreciate the range of ethnic identities in the UK.

Chinese New Year

What you need
Art materials; envelopes; pictures of Chinese New Year celebrations, including dragons; cooked rice; spring onions; soya sauce; beansprouts; carrots; ginger and garlic; oil; a wok; bowls and chopsticks. See: www.activityvillage.co.uk/chinese_new_year.htm

Background
Chinese New Year is celebrated between 1 January and 19 February. There are 12 different names for each New Year, used in a 12-year cycle. This is based on a legend. When Buddha was about to leave the Earth, only 12 animals came to say goodbye. As a reward a year was named after each one. There was a contest to see who headed the names. All the animals had to cross a river and the first to arrive on the other side would head the list. The ox was winning but the rat had travelled on his back and jumped on to the bank first. The names of the years are: Rat, Ox, Tiger, Rabbit, Dragon, Snake, Horse, Goat, Monkey, Rooster, Dog and Pig.

To celebrate New Year, Chinese homes are cleaned and decorated with red banners and streamers, hanging lanterns, red envelopes with money in them and squares of bright paper decorated with words such as 'happiness', 'wealth' and 'longevity'. Lots of food is eaten and there are fireworks to scare away evil spirits.

What to do
● Explain to the children the background to Chinese New Year.
● You could prepare the classroom to look like a Chinese home.
● When you leave school on Chinese New Year's Eve, seal the door on the outside as you leave with masking tape. (Remember to tell the cleaners and other school staff!)
● On Chinese New Year's Day, ask a child to take off the seal before anyone goes into the classroom.
● Check with parents and carers first for any food allergies or dietary requirements, then make a simple stir-fry using cooked rice mixed with vegetables. (Ensure that the rice is kept refrigerated until it is needed.) Children can help cut the spring onions and carrots into thin julienne strips (being very careful with the knives), then all the ingredients are stir-fried in a wok with a little oil and soya sauce until still crisp but tender.
● The children can enjoy eating it in little bowls with chopsticks.

Differentiation
More able children could do further research into different Chinese traditions and write each one on separate sheets to use as a display.

St Valentine's Day

AGE RANGE 7–11

LEARNING OBJECTIVES
To understand more about the traditions of St Valentine's Day and to produce some artwork based on those traditions.

CURRICULUM LINKS
Art and design: KS2 2c – to use a variety of methods and approaches to communicate ideas, and to design and make images.

What you need
Paper; card; paints; pastels; a box for all the cards.

Background
The date of 14 February is linked to the Roman feast of *Lupercalia* when the names of girls were placed into jars and each boy drew one out. This girl would be the boy's partner for the whole of the feast. According to the early Christian church, St Valentine – who was martyred on 14 February 269 AD – left a note for his jailer's daughter saying 'From your Valentine'; and so this became the day for exchanging love messages. There are lots of other Valentine's Day traditions. For example, young men in Tudor times would draw women's names from a bowl and wear that name stuck to their sleeves for a week. Men carved love spoons out of wood in Wales, decorated them with keys, keyholes and hearts, and gave them to their sweethearts. In some countries, young women would receive a gift of clothing from young men. If a young woman kept the gift then she would marry the boy. If a young woman saw a robin she would marry a sailor; a sparrow and she would marry a poor man, but be very happy; if she saw a goldfinch, she would marry a rich man. If a girl cut an apple in half and counted the number of seeds (pips) inside she would know how many children she would have. The first young man a young girl saw on Valentine's Day would be the person she would marry.

What to do
● Ask the children what they think St Valentine's Day means and then tell them about the background to 14 February.
● Ask them to work in pairs and illustrate one of the traditions. These can be used as a wall display.
● Ask each child to make small Valentine's card and write a kind message inside but remember – no names should be used.
● Place the cards in a box. Each child picks one out and guesses who it is from.

Differentiation
More able children can do further research about the history of Valentine's Day and write it for the class book.

World Thinking Day

AGE RANGE 5–7

LEARNING OBJECTIVES
To discover more about World Thinking Day and to begin to understand more about being healthy and healthy eating.

CURRICULUM LINKS
Science: QCA Unit 2A 'Health and growth' – to recognise that an adequate diet and exercise are necessary to stay healthy.

What you need
Real examples (or pictures) of healthy and unhealthy foods, see www.healthyliving.gov.uk; commercial charts that divide food types into healthy and less healthy; apples, oranges, carrots and celery; honey and yoghurt.

Background
World Thinking Day was created in 1926 and is celebrated on 22 February. This is the joint birthday of Lord and Lady Baden Powell who founded the Scout and Guide movement.

What to do
● Link the issues of thinking and healthy food choices.
● Divide the whiteboard into two halves – 'Healthy food' and 'Unhealthy food'. Tell the children what the day is about and ask them what they think are healthy foods. List these in the healthy half. Ask them to say what are unhealthy foods, which they should not eat too much of – and list them.
● Discuss why we should eat more healthy foods (keep us fit, give us energy, healthy skin and shiny hair).
● Ask what happens if we eat too many unhealthy foods (we are unfit, get obese, not able to run around, more illnesses).
● Show real examples of healthy foods – or use photographs. Hold them up and ask what each one is because some children may not recognise potatoes, leeks and so on. Ask whether each food is healthy – and if we can eat a lot of this food – or unhealthy and we should not eat too much of it.
● Chocolate, ice cream and crisps are not healthy but you need to stress that it is OK to eat them occasionally because they are very tasty.
● Cut the apples, oranges, celery and carrot into small slices and ask the children to either eat them on their own or dip them into the honey or the yoghurt.
● Divide a display board into half and label it 'Green for Go' on one side and 'Red for Stop' on the other.
● The children can either paint or draw pictures of healthy foods or find pictures and stick them on the Green side with a label, or do the same with unhealthy food and stick them on the Red side.

Differentiation
More able children can write out reasons for certain foods being unhealthy and could produce a menu for a healthy meal.

AGE RANGE 5–8

LEARNING OBJECTIVES
To understand some of the customs of Shrove Tuesday and its relationship to Lent and Easter.

CURRICULUM LINKS
Design and technology: KS1 and KS2 5c – to carry out assignments using food.

Shrove Tuesday

What you need
Copies of 'Making pancakes' photocopiable page 51; ingredients for pancakes; ingredients for fillings.

Background
Shrove Tuesday was part of the three or four days known as Shrovetide. It is the last day following Christmas when Christians used to eat well and enjoy themselves because it is followed by Lent, the period of 40 days of fasting and repentance leading up to Easter. Few Christians now fast for Lent, but many give up small luxuries. Shrove comes from the old word 'shrive' meaning confess. Many Christians would confess their sins so that they were forgiven before Lent began. Shrovetide used to be celebrated with games, sports and dancing and football was played in the streets. Shrove Tuesday itself used to be a half-day holiday and church bells would ring to tell everyone to stop work. The last of the fat, butter and eggs were used up, which may be why pancakes are traditionally made and why Shrove Tuesday is also known as Pancake Day. Even the pancakes became part of the festival and, in some villages, the first pancake cooked has to be given to the chickens so that they carry on through the year laying eggs. In other parts of the country, the first three pancakes made had to be marked with a cross and stored in a tin to ward off evil spirits during the next year. There are also pancake races where the runners must carry frying pans and toss their pancakes at least three times during the race.

What to do
● Discuss and talk about the reasons for celebrating Shrove Tuesday and some of the old customs.
● Check with parents and carers first for any food allergies or dietary requirements, then use photocopiable page 51 to make pancakes. The recipe will make about 12 so for a whole class you will need to adjust the ingredients.
● Children could also think about different pancake fillings, which could be sweet or savoury.
● Ask them to work in pairs or small groups to choose one sweet and one savoury filling and make a list of the ingredients.
● They could use their own fillings for their pancakes – or sample each other's.

Differentiation
More able children can do further research into old customs and could write about and illustrate some of these for Lent and Shrove Tuesday.

A summary of some of the Universal Declaration of Human Rights

Children should be born free and should act towards one another in a friendly manner;

You have the right to live in freedom and safety;

Nobody has the right to treat you as a slave or to torture you;

Laws should be available to protect you;

Nobody has the right to put you in prison unjustly;

If you are accused of a crime you should be considered innocent until proved guilty and tried in a public place;

You have the right to be protected if someone is threatening you with harm;

You have the right to travel to other countries and to return safely to your own;

You have the right to marry who you want to and not to be forced into marrying anyone;

You have a right to own things and no one has the right to take them from you without good reason;

You have the right to practise your religion freely and without harm;

You should be able to vote and to take part in the government of your country;

You have the right to work and to be paid a fair wage;

You have the right to be educated and to go to school;

You should be able to learn a profession and continue your education and develop your talents;

No one should be allowed to destroy the rights that are listed here.

Office of the High Commission for Human Rights: http://www.ohchr.org

Designing a nativity scene

● When you have completed this sheet discuss what you are going to do with an adult.

● Draw the outside of your design.

● List the materials you will need to construct the outside on to your shoe box.

_____

_____

● Draw the nativity scene inside the box.

● List the materials you will need.

_____

_____

● Are there any problems you can think of, or any difficulties?

_____

_____

Templates for the nativity scene

Burns Night

Part of a poem by Robert Burns

● Try reading it to yourself and to a partner and with your partner or group explain what it means.

> Wee, sleekit, cow'rin, tim'rous beastie,
> O, what panics in thy breastie!
> Thou need na start awa sae hasty,
> Wi' bickering brattle!
> I wad be laith to rin an' chase thee,
> Wi' murd'rin pattle

● Cut along the above line and give to the poem to the children

● Here is what some of the words mean

sleekit: sleek

cow'rin: cowering

tim'rous   timorous

bickering brattle: hurrying scamper

laith: loth

pattle: long handled spade

The title of the poem is: **To a Mouse**

Making pancakes

● Note: Make sure that everyone is aware of health and safety issues – especially children and any volunteer adults who may be needed to help make the pancakes. The pans get very hot! Someone will have to toss a pancake – an adult should do this.

Pancake batter

110g plain flour
pinch of salt
2 large organic free range eggs
200ml milk mixed with 75ml water
2 tablespoons melted butter or oil
extra butter or oil for cooking the pancakes

● Mix the flour with the salt in a large mixing bowl.

● Make a well in the centre of the flour and break the two eggs into it.

● Whisk the eggs with a whisk or fork, drawing in flour from the edges.

● Start adding the milk/water mix and continue adding and whisking until you have a smooth batter. It should be the consistency of single cream.

● When you are ready to cook, stir in the melted butter or oil to the batter.

● Melt a small amount of butter or oil in a frying pan and make sure the whole of the surface is just coated in butter or oil – not swimming in it.

● Get the pan really hot, turn the heat to medium and drop in two tablespoons of the batter.

● Quickly swirl it round so it spreads in the pan to make a pancake. Cook for about half a minute until browned on the bottom. This is the time to toss it if you are going to try. If it is thin, it will not need turning over.

● Slide it onto a plate and eat straight away or keep warm until all the pancakes are cooked.

● Serve the pancakes with jam, lemon juice and sugar or golden syrup, or whatever topping you think will be best.

Spring

March to May

AGE RANGE 5–11

LEARNING OBJECTIVES
To understand the importance of Ash Wednesday and its links to Shrove Tuesday and Lent.

CURRICULUM LINKS
Religious education: QCA Unit 1D 'Beliefs and practice' – to understand that festivals are celebrations of symbolic significance for believers; Unit 4C 'Why is Easter important to Christians?' – to learn about the events of Palm Sunday.

Ash Wednesday

What you need
Sheets of A5 paper (half an A4 sheet) each; writing and drawing materials.

Background
Lent begins with Ash Wednesday, the day after Shrove Tuesday, and lasts for 40 days until Easter Sunday. Jesus spent 40 days in the wilderness praying and fasting and Christians imitate this period by giving up something they like doing or something they enjoy eating. Christians believe that giving up good and enjoyable things for a while encourages self-discipline and humility and reminds them of the importance of spiritual goods over earthly goods.

In the past (and still in some churches today) a small amount of ash was smeared on each worshipper's forehead. Traditionally, the ashes were made from burning the palm crosses that had been used in the church during last year's Palm Sunday and mixing the ashes with holy water. On Ash Wednesday, in some villages in the north of England, children would put twigs that they broke from ash trees down their socks. Children who did not do this could have their foot stamped on!

What to do
● Discuss Shrove Tuesday with the children and the background to Ash Wednesday.
● Remind them about the meaning of Lent.
● Talk about pancakes and how they used up ingredients which were not meant to be eaten during Lent, such as fat, butter and eggs.
● Ask the children to help make a list of all the food that they would not be able to eat, if their parents stopped using these ingredients from now until Easter.
● Talk about how difficult it is to give up something you like by relating it to New Year's Resolutions and how hard it can be to keep them.
● Ask the children to tell you what they could try to give up. This can range from food, such as crisps or chocolate, to doing things like playing computer games or watching certain programmes on television. List them all.
● Ask the children each to write down one of these resolutions on the small sheets of paper and illustrate it in bright colours.
● Mount the finished pictures on a display board with the title 'What I would find difficult to give up for Lent'.

Differentiation
More able children could write down reasons why it is difficult to give things up – why it is difficult to go without favourite foods and activities.

AGE RANGE 5–7

LEARNING OBJECTIVES
To understand who St David was and why St David's day is celebrated.

CURRICULUM LINKS
Religious education: QCA Unit 2C 'Celebrations' – to understand that festivals are occasions for remembering particular events.
Art and design: Unit 2B 'Mother Nature, designer' – to record natural objects from first-hand observation.

St David's Day

What you need
Good quality drawing paper; a selection of pencils; leeks and daffodils (enough for each child to be able to look at closely).

Background
St David's Day is celebrated on 1 March in honour of the patron saint of Wales. David was a Celtic monk who lived 1400 years ago. He spread the message of Christianity across Wales. He was very good at speaking to large groups of people and teaching them about Christianity. One day he was talking in a valley and he was concerned that he could not be seen or heard. As David spoke, the ground rose up under his feet until he was standing on a hill where everyone could see him. David was once asked to help fight off an invading army in a narrow valley where there was very little space to move. As the soldiers on both sides were wearing very similar clothes it was difficult to tell them apart. David told the defending soldiers to pull up the leeks that were growing in the fields and stick them in their helmets. They did this and so could tell who was on their side. The Welsh army won the battle and, on St David's Day now, soldiers in Welsh regiments are presented with leeks. St David's Day is not celebrated in any noisy or colourful way. But it is a day when Welsh people from all over the world think about their country and what it means to them to be Welsh.

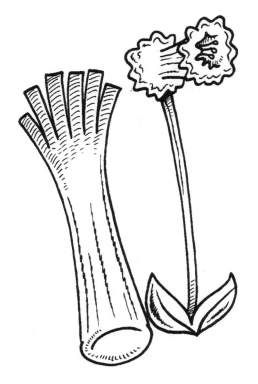

What to do
● First of all discuss with the children what they think 'saints' are and what makes them special.
● Talk about the background to St David's Day and read them the legends about St David. Discuss what 'legends' are and find out whether the children know of any other similar legends, for example St George and the dragon.
● Show the children the daffodil and the leek. Both of them are national emblems of Wales.
● Ask them to look carefully at a leek and a daffodil and to do a close observational drawing of each one to be displayed in the classroom.

Differentiation
More able children could do further research and write up the legends in prose or as poetry, or even as a newspaper report.

AGE RANGE 7–11

LEARNING OBJECTIVES
To understand why this day is important and to recognise the achievements of women in the past and present.

CURRICULUM LINKS
History: QCA Unit 20 'What can we learn about recent history from studying the life of a famous person?' – to select information to represent key aspects of a biography; to begin to evaluate the impact of an individual on our lives today.

International Women's Day

What you need
Access to books and the internet for research; copies of 'Interview sheet' photocopiable page 73; paper for writing and drawing.

Background
International Women's Day, on 8 March, celebrates the achievements of women and girls and is also an opportunity to continue to speak out against the inequalities they face. For example: women account for 70 per cent of the world's population who live in poverty; 65 million girls currently do not go to school. The United Nations makes it clear that social progress and world peace require the active participation and equality of women and that until the full potential and rights of women and girls are achieved, lasting solutions to the world's most serious social, economic and political problems are unlikely to be found.

What to do
● Before International Women's Day make sure that every child completes the 'Interview sheet' – photocopiable page 73.
● Discuss the background to International Women's Day, including the children's views on inequality.
● Give the girls the opportunity to discuss how they feel about equality, especially in school – there may be surprise answers!
● Discuss their findings from the interviews they carried out. The most interesting and challenging comments can be used as a display.
● Talk about who they think are famous women – include some from history and from the present. Make sure they are women who have made a difference in some way, such as:
Marie Curie, Emily Pankhurst, Kelly Holmes and current women politicians, rather than just 'celebrities' such as pop stars.
● Decide who the children think are the five or six most important and make a display. They could either illustrate some of the women's activities or use newspaper and magazine articles of famous women and write a summary of their achievements.
● The writing should include what each woman has done that is important and also why the children feel that they should be celebrated on International Women's day.

Differentiation
Less able children might find some of the concepts difficult. They may also need help in interviewing someone, perhaps they could interview a teaching assistant or teacher. More able children should do further in-depth research.

Festivals

AGE RANGE 5–11

LEARNING OBJECTIVES
To raise children's awareness of the wider world and their own place in it.

CURRICULUM LINKS
Geography: KS1 and KS2 2c – to use maps in a range of scales.
Citizenship: QCA Unit 5 'Living in a diverse world' – to recognise that there are similarities and differences between communities in other parts of the world and our own.

Commonwealth Day

What you need

Paints and felt-tipped pens; large map of the world; coloured pictures of the flags of Commonwealth countries, see: www.commonwealthday.co.uk

Background

Commonwealth Day is an annual celebration held on the second Monday in March. The modern Commonwealth is made up of 1.8 billion people in 53 countries. This is 30 per cent of the world's population. There is a special service in Westminster Abbey attended by the Queen, who also broadcasts a Commonwealth message. The day is celebrated in many different ways but the main emphasis is always on the unity of different countries, races and religions.

What to do

● Find out what the children know about the Commonwealth and explain the background information.
● Make sure that the large map of the world is mounted on an even larger display board. Ask the children if they know where some of the Commonwealth countries are and show them.
● Research and cut out pictures of the flags for all of the 53 Commonwealth countries.
● Divide the children into groups of four and allocate one or two countries to each group. Ask them to locate the country on the large map and attach each flag to the display board with a length of cotton leading it to its country.
● Give the children access to the internet and to the library. They should find out some basic information about their country, such as the capital city and industries, which can be used for a display. They could also find out:

    1. What food is typical of the country? Could we make it?
    2. Are there any popular children's games? Could we play them?

● The information can be used to hold a Commonwealth Games or Commonwealth cooking day at school.
● Find out from other classes if any of the children have links with Commonwealth countries. Prepare some statistics or graphs, for example: 'Which Commonwealth country does this school have the most links with?'

Differentiation

More able children could do further research and prepare detailed profiles of countries. Less able children will need help to find countries and to locate them on the world map.

AGE RANGE 5–11

LEARNING OBJECTIVES
To understand more about St Patrick and why he is associated with Ireland.

CURRICULUM LINKS
NLS: Y3 T3 Text 22 – to experiment with recounting the same event in a variety of ways; Y5 T2 Text 11 – to write own versions of legends.
Art and design: QCA Unit 2B 'Mother Nature, designer' – investigate different patterns of snakeskins.

St Patrick's Day

What you need
Art materials; paper; Plasticine or clay (optional); books about St Patrick.

Background
St Patrick is the patron saint of Ireland and St Patrick's Day is 17 March. It is celebrated in a happy and noisy fashion by Irish people all over the world who wear shamrocks (similar to a clover plant) and take part in parades, music and singing. There are a lot of facts known about St Patrick. He was born in Britain but his father was a Roman. Patrick was originally a pagan and he was taken to Ireland as a slave, but he escaped and then became a Christian, going back to Ireland as a priest and later becoming a bishop. He played a major part in converting the Irish to Christianity. St Patrick was also supposed to have banished all snakes from Ireland. This is more likely to be a legend because there were probably never any snakes in Ireland. In many old pagan religions snakes and serpents were common and often worshipped. So the story about driving out the snakes from Ireland is more likely to be about driving out pagan practices. St Patrick is believed to have died on 17 March. One account says

he died in Ireland, where his jaw bone is preserved in a silver shrine. Another account says that he died in England at Glastonbury Abbey, where there is a Chapel of St Patrick.

What to do
● Find out from the children what they know about St Patrick and St Patrick's Day.
● Discuss and talk about 'legends' and 'truth' and what the differences are between saints and ordinary people.
● Tell the children about St Patrick's background and what is known about his life.
● There are two main symbols – the shamrock and banishing snakes.
● Ask the children to use their imagination and draw and paint large, imaginary snakes. They could also use Plasticine or clay to make snakes of all shapes and sizes.
● Some children could write accounts of St Patrick's life and these can be displayed alongside the observational drawings and models.

Differentiation
More able children will be able to use the written stories about St Patrick to produce their own accounts of his life. For older children this could be in the form of an obituary.

AGE RANGE 5–7

LEARNING OBJECTIVES
To understand more about Purim and the story behind the festival.

CURRICULUM LINKS
Religious education: QCA Unit 1D 'Beliefs and practice' – to understand that festivals are celebrations of symbolic significance for believers; Unit 2C 'Celebrations' – to understand that festivals are occasions for remembering particular events. Design and technology: KS1 2d – to assemble and join components accurately.

Purim

What you need
Materials to make a 'gragger' including:
cardboard tubes, card, dried peas or rice; copies of 'The story of Purim' and 'Make your own gragger' photocopiable pages 74 and 75.

Background
Purim is one of the liveliest and most entertaining of Jewish holidays. It celebrates the time when the Jewish people were saved by a young woman called Esther. It is usually held in the first weeks of March and there is lots of eating and drinking. Baskets of sweets, fruit, nuts, bagels and wine are sold and there are different types of pastries to eat. There are also carnivals and parades. One of the most important events during Purim is when the story of Esther is told in the synagogue. It is a noisy and rowdy occasion. The synagogue is crowded and many children dress up in costumes and masks. The Purim story has an evil character called Haman and, during the storytelling, everyone in the synagogue boos, hisses and rattles their 'graggers' whenever Haman's name is mentioned.

What to do
● Talk about the background to Purim and tell the children that they will be making 'graggers'.
● 'Graggers' make a rattling noise. Ask the children to think about what objects they might use to make this sound.
● Let the children work in small groups to experiment with various objects and containers to see which make the loudest rattle.
● They can then use photocopiable page 75 to design their own gragger. The children may want to substitute dried peas for some of the materials they tested earlier.
● The children should plan how they will decorate them, stressing that the graggers should be as bright and colourful as possible.
● The children can then make their instruments. These can be used to accompany a retelling of the story of Esther on photocopiable page 74. Remind the children that they must rattle their 'graggers' to make as much noise as possible every time Haman's name is mentioned.

Differentiation
More able children will be able to write their own version of the story of Esther or they could write their own instructions for making a gragger. Less able children will need help making their graggers.

AGE RANGE 5–7

LEARNING OBJECTIVES
To understand more about the Hindu festival of Holi and to develop some ideas about the Hindu religion.

CURRICULUM LINKS
Religious education: QCA Unit 1D 'Beliefs and practice' – to understand that festivals are celebrations of symbolic significance for believers; Unit 2C 'Celebrations' – to understand that festivals are occasions for remembering particular events.

Holi

What you need
Large and small art paper; coloured tissue paper; small pieces of writing paper; pictures of Hindu gods.

Background
Holi is the Hindu festival in March that celebrates spring and new life. It is a joyful and lively festival filled with fun and good humour. There is singing and dancing and people smear each other with paint. Lots of food is cooked and, because of the story of Prahlad and Holika, bonfires are lit to keep away evil spirits.

Prahlad was the son of a king who wanted everyone to worship him. But Prahlad refused to worship his father. Instead he continued to worship Lord Vishnu. The king's sister, Holika, who was immune to fire, tricked Prahlad into sitting on her lap in the middle of a huge bonfire. He walked away unharmed because he was good. She was using her powers for evil and perished in the flames.

What to do
● Talk to the children about what happens in spring and look for signs around the school. If possible, you could bring in daffodils and catkins.
● Talk about the background to Holi and discuss what happens in the festival.
● Explain that Hindus believe that there are different sides of the same god, and that there are many different gods such as Krishna, Lakshmi and Ganesha.
● Ask the children to draw a picture of themselves, cut it out and stick it in the middle of a larger piece of paper.
● Talk about how everyone has several different 'sides' or aspects of their personalities. Sometimes we are happy, sometimes sad, angry and so on.
● Ask the children to write a sentence about each of their different sides and stick them around their picture of themselves. Each sentence could start in the same way: *'Sometimes I am…'*
● The children can cut out shapes of coloured tissue paper, decorate them with glitter and sequins representing the bright colours of Holi, and use the shapes to surround their pictures.

Differentiation
More able children could do some further research, then write about and draw different Hindu gods and rewrite the story of Prahlad and Holika. Less able children will need support with their writing.

AGE RANGE 5–11

LEARNING OBJECTIVES
To understand why Mothering Sunday is a special day and to learn more about its history.

CURRICULUM LINKS
PSHE and citizenship: KS1 1b – to share opinions on things that matter to them and explain their views. Religious education: KS2 2e – to reflect on sources of inspiration in their own lives.

Mothering Sunday

What you need
Plain writing paper; drawing paper and materials; a food mixing bowl; a large spoon; copies of 'What is special about my mother?' photocopiable page 76.

Background
Mothering Sunday is celebrated on the fourth Sunday in Lent. It was originally a religious festival when servants and apprentices were given a day off work to go back to the place where they were born to visit their 'mother church'. This meant it became a family reunion day. Many people began to bring flowers and other treats for their mothers and sometimes a special cake called a Simnel cake was made. Nowadays it is when children recognise how important their mothers are and give them gifts and cards.

What to do
● Talk to the children about the background to Mothering Sunday, reminding them about Lent.
● Ask them what special things they do on Mothering Sunday. These 'special' things could be written on small pieces of paper and mounted on a display board.
● Talk about what is special about mothers. What do they do that is important? Why do they deserve a special day? Write down these ideas on small pieces of paper. Remember that this can be a very sensitive area if some children do not have mothers or have difficult family relationships.
● Explain that you are going to make an imaginary Simnel cake.
● The ingredients are: a cup of 'kindness'; a tablespoon of 'happiness'; a pinch of 'being funny'; a kilogram of 'good times' and a teaspoon of 'caring'.
● Stand with the bowl and large spoon to stir the mixture. Ask the children to bring their pieces of paper to the front and read them out before put them in the 'cake mix'; for example *happiness* might include 'reading to me', and *good times* might include 'going on holiday together'.
● Ask the children to use the photocopiable sheet as a writing frame for what they think makes their mother special. They can include examples from the imaginary Simnel cake.
● Display the writing on the 'special things' board.
● They should draw portraits of their mothers and mount these on their Mothering Sunday display.

A tablespoon of happiness
A cup of kindness
A teaspoon of caring

Differentiation
More able children could find a recipe for Simnel cake and everyone could help make it.

AGE RANGE 5–11

LEARNING OBJECTIVES
To understand more about the traditions and history of April (All) Fools Day.

CURRICULUM LINKS
PSHE and citizenship: KS2 2k – to explore how the media present information.
NLS: Y2 T3 Text 20 – to write non-fiction text, using texts read as models for own writing; Y4 T3 Text 25 – to design an advertisement.

April or All Fool's Day

What you need
Writing and drawing paper; pencils and crayons; newspapers for 1 April (optional).

Background
April Fool's or All Fool's Day on 1 April is when people play tricks on each other. No one really knows when the custom started but it might have been because of the change in calendars in 1582. This is complicated but in the old Julian calendar, New Year was celebrated from 25 March until 1 April. The first day of the new Gregorian calendar (which we still use today) became 1 January. In France some people forgot and still celebrated New Year on 1 April. Other people would play tricks on them and call them April Fools. Now, many newspapers and even television programmes often try to fool people with spoof news items. Some years ago a television programme persuaded people that spaghetti grew on trees and that there was going to be a bumper crop. There was also a report on dehydrated water which was a powder that needed light to turn it into liquid. There were pictures of flooding caused by a lorry full of the powder overturning in bright sunshine and spilling into the road. BMW had a newspaper advert for a car with pedals on both sides and a detachable steering wheel – so that it could be easily driven in France and Britain.

In many countries playing tricks only lasts until noon. After 12 o'clock you can turn round and say:
'April fool is dead and gone
You're the fool to carry it on'.

What to do
● Talk about the background to April Fool's Day and ask the children to talk about some of their favourite tricks.
● Discuss the fact that 'serious' radio and television programmes and newspapers can also play tricks on April Fool's Day and tell the children about some of them.
● Ask the children to make up their own April Fool advertisements – remind them that while it has to be ridiculous it also needs to be just about believable.

Differentiation
More able children can read the newspapers to see whether they can find this year's April Fool's trick.

World Health Day

AGE RANGE 5–11

LEARNING OBJECTIVES
To identify what we eat and how it can contribute to a healthy lifestyle.

CURRICULUM LINKS
Science: QCA Unit 2A 'Health and growth'; Unit 3A 'Teeth and eating'; Unit 5A 'Keeping healthy' – to recognise that an adequate and varied diet are needed to keep healthy.

What you need
Copies of 'Balancing your food' and 'Food groups' photocopiable pages 77 and 78; writing and drawing materials; red, green and yellow highlighter pens.

Background
World Health Day is held on 7 April. This day is intended to encourage governments, communities and individuals to take action to improve health and well being. Its main aims are: to raise awareness of the problems of ill health across the world; to increase understanding that there are solutions that will prevent illness and that all communities and countries must take more action to prevent illness and ill health.

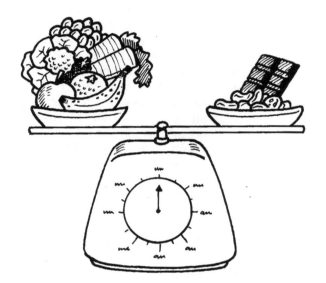

What to do
● Talk to the children about the purpose of World Health Day. Use examples such as hunger in Africa and diseases like malaria.
● Tell the children that they will be looking at how to maintain their healthy lifestyles by eating the right foods. Explain the problems with obesity and heart disease.
● The day before, ask the children to note down and list everything they eat and drink.
● The next day, split the children into groups and ask them to discuss the foods and drinks on their lists. Give the children a copy of the 'Balancing your food' photocopiable sheet and encourage them to work out which sections the foods on their list comes from.
● With high-energy food, try not to classify them as unhealthy. Instead, talk about how foods in this category give us a quick burst of energy and are then used up. Having a small amount from this section will give lots of energy for running around at playtime, but will later leave them hungry unless they have eaten food from the other energy section, which releases energy more slowly.
● Ask each group to share some of their results with the rest of the class.
● Explain that part of being healthy is eating a balanced diet which is a combination of different food groups. Give the children examples of different meals, for example, cheese and tomato sandwich, packet of crisps and orange juice. Using the 'Balancing your food' photocopiable sheet, ask the children to write down or draw where each of different foods from the meal would go on the 'Food groups' photocopiable sheet. What could they add to the meal to ensure that they are eating a balanced diet?
● Ask the children to think of one thing each to improve their diet. These can be illustrated and used as part of a healthy eating display.
● Challenge the children to do what they have suggested. Check in a week's time.

Differentiation
More able children could write out a full day's meals that will promote good health. Less able children will need support throughout this activity, especially in making choices between foods.

Palm Sunday

AGE RANGE 5–11

LEARNING OBJECTIVES
To understand more about the meaning of Palm Sunday and why it is a special day in the Christian calendar.

CURRICULUM LINKS
Religious education: QCA Unit 1D 'Beliefs and practice' – to understand that festivals are celebrations of symbolic significance for believers; Unit 4C 'Why is Easter important to Christians?' – to learn about the events of Palm Sunday.
Art and design: KS1 and KS2 2c – to design and make images.

What you need
Paper for a freeze; painting and drawing materials; other art materials for individual figures and trees.

Background
For Christians, Palm Sunday marks the beginning of Holy Week – the week before Easter and which ends the period of Lent. It celebrates the day when Jesus entered Jerusalem for the feast of Pesach. As Jesus came into the city he was cheered by an excited crowd who believed that he was the Messiah. They waved palm branches to welcome him, spread branches on the road and shouted 'Hosanna' which means 'save us now'. In England, people who go to church are given palm crosses and some churches will have a procession around the church and will sing songs and wave their palm crosses. Any leftover palm crosses will be burnt and used to make the ash for next year's Ash Wednesday.

What to do
● Remind the children about Lent and talk to them about the background to Palm Sunday. The story is in the New Testament in Mark 11: 1–11, Mathew 21: 1–11 and Luke 19: 28–38.
● It is important to contrast the happy and excited feelings of the crowd and how Jesus would be feeling, knowing that he was soon to die.
● Ask the children if they have ever been in a crowd or a procession and find out how they felt. If they have been to a football match they should know a lot about how crowds react.
● Start making a freeze of Jesus' procession into Jerusalem.
● First of all, the children should draw and colour the houses and trees and mount them on the freeze paper. If you want to be ambitious some of them could be 3D. At the same time, stick straw along the road to represent the palm branches.
● Draw and colour lots of figures with brightly coloured clothes and all with different faces. Many will need to be waving palm leaves.
● Draw and colour Jesus on his donkey with his disciples.
● Mount all the figures on the freeze, making sure that the crowd looks as if it contains lots of people

Differentiation
More able children could read the story from the Bible and rewrite it from the point of view of someone in the crowd or a Roman centurion.

AGE RANGE 5–11

LEARNING OBJECTIVES
To understand more about what Maundy Thursday
means and why it is celebrated.

CURRICULUM LINKS
Religious education: QCA Unit 1D 'Beliefs and
practice' – to understand that festivals are celebrations
of symbolic significance for believers; Unit 4C 'Why is
Easter important to Christians?' – to learn about the
Last Supper.

Maundy Thursday

What you need
A print of Leonardo da Vinci's *The Last Supper*; large sheets of paper that can be divided
into eight sections to create a comic strip; pencils, rulers and crayons.

Background
Maundy Thursday is the day before Good Friday; when Christians remember the Last
Supper – the last time Jesus and his disciples all ate together. The night of Maundy
Thursday was also when Judas betrayed Jesus in the Garden of Gethsemane. The word
'Maundy' probably comes from the Latin word *maundatum* meaning 'command'
because Jesus told his disciples at the Last Supper: 'And now I give you a new
command: love one another. As I have loved you, so must you love one another.' Jesus
also washed the feet of all his disciples. According to tradition, on Maundy Thursday the
king or queen used to wash the feet of a few selected people. Now, the Queen gives
away Maundy Money. The number of men and the number of women who receive the
money equal the age of the Queen.

What to do
● Talk to the children about the background to Maundy Thursday and show them the
picture of the Last Supper.
● Discuss the meaning of friends and friendship. Try to find some key descriptive words
and phrases, for example, loyal, share secrets, having the same interests.
● Talk about Judas betraying Jesus for money and discuss what betrayal means to
them. Link it to friends by asking such questions as, 'How would you feel if one of your
friends was unkind and disloyal?' 'What sort of things might a disloyal friend do?'
● Ask them to work in pairs, choose whether they want to write a comic strip called
'close friends' or one called 'betrayed by a friend' and then discuss the types of stories
they could produce.
● Remind them about comics and such devices as
speech bubbles and think bubbles.
● The children need to divide their paper
into eight equal sections and then create
their own comic strip. These could be
put on a display board for all to see.

Differentiation
Many children will need help in
dividing their paper into eight
sections. More able children can find
the appropriate sections in the Bible
and read them to the class.

AGE RANGE 5–11

LEARNING OBJECTIVES
To understand more about the meaning of Good Friday and how it is linked to the rest of the Easter Festival.

CURRICULUM LINKS
Religious education: QCA Unit 1D 'Beliefs and practice' – to understand that festivals are celebrations of symbolic significance for believers; Unit 4C 'Why is Easter important to Christians?' – to understand why the cross is an important symbols for Christians.

Good Friday

What you need
Paper and writing materials; hot cross buns.

Background
Good Friday is the Friday before Easter Sunday and is the day when Christians remember the crucifixion of Jesus. The name could come from 'God's Friday' but another old name for the day was 'Long Friday' because many Christians fasted all day. Jesus was innocent of all the crimes he was tried for. He was blameless and Pontius Pilate the Roman governor knew this but gave Jesus to the crowds who beat him, placed a crown of thorns on his head and made him carry his cross to a hill called *Golgotha* – Skull Hill. He was nailed to the cross between two thieves and mocked as the King of the Jews. When Jesus died he was placed in a tomb like a cave and huge rocks were placed across the entrance.

Warm 'hot cross buns' are eaten on Good Friday and the cross on the top is a symbol of the crucifixion. There are also several superstitions. It was believed that bread, cakes or hot cross buns baked on Good Friday had magic properties and would not go mouldy. These hard buns were supposed to protect the house from fire and sailors would take them to sea to prevent shipwreck. It was also thought that the hard hot cross buns could be grated into warm milk to make upset stomachs better.

What to do
- Talk about and discuss the background to Good Friday.
- Ask the children whether they go to church over Easter and what happens.
- Discuss some of the Good Friday traditions and ask whether they eat hot cross buns.
- Ask the children to discuss these questions in groups:
    1. Have you ever been blamed for something you didn't do?
    2. Did you have to face the consequences?
    3. How did you feel?
- Ask them to write a paragraph answering the questions and read some of them out to the class.
- End the day by sharing together the hot cross buns.

Differentiation
More able children could write longer accounts and look up the Easter story in the Bible. Less able children will need lots of support with the writing.

Easter Sunday

AGE RANGE 5–11

LEARNING OBJECTIVES
To understand more about the meaning of Easter Sunday and how it links into the rest of the Easter festival.

CURRICULUM LINKS
Religious education: QCA Unit 1D 'Beliefs and practice' – to understand that festivals are celebrations of symbolic significance for believers; Unit 4C 'Why is Easter important to Christians?' – to think about why Christians believe in life after death.

What you need
Art paper; hard-boiled eggs or blown eggs; words and music to the hymn 'There is a green hill far away'; felt-tipped pens, paints and inks.

Background
Easter Sunday is an extremely important day in the Christian calendar as it celebrates Jesus rising from the dead. Christians all over the world celebrate the resurrection of Jesus. On the Sunday morning after Good Friday a group of women went to Jesus' tomb and found that the rock which had been placed across the entrance had been rolled aside. Suddenly there was a bright light and Jesus was standing in front of them. He told them that he had risen from the dead and that they should go and tell all the other disciples. Some of the disciples didn't believe what was happening but later in the day Jesus came into the room where they all were and spoke to them and showed them the wounds in his hands and feet.

Eggs are a traditional Easter food and chocolate eggs are given as gifts. This is because eggs are symbols of new life and also eating eggs was forbidden during Lent. The Greeks and Egyptians both buried eggs in their tombs. Gifts of eggs probably started out as real eggs that had been painted in bright colours which were supposed to be the colours of spring.

What to do
● Discuss with the children the background to Easter Sunday and how it fits into Lent and the festival of Easter.
● Ask them about how they celebrate Easter at home and what they like best about it.
● Explain that they will be decorating their own eggs with bright colours and intricate patterns.
● First of all ask them to design and colour their patterns on the drawing paper. These will make a good display.
● Give each child an egg to decorate – but have plenty of spares in case they get broken.
● There could be a competition for the best decorated egg and they could be displayed for other classes to see.
● Teach the children to sing a verse of 'There is a green hill far away'.

Differentiation
More able children could use the Bible to find the story of the resurrection and read it to the class.

AGE RANGE 7–11

LEARNING OBJECTIVES
To understand the importance and the background to the Sikh festival of Baisakhi.

CURRICULUM OBJECTIVES
Religious education: KS2 1b – to describe the variety of practices and ways of life in religions and understand how these stem from, and are closely connected, to beliefs and teachings; 2a – to reflect on what it means to belong to a faith community.

Baisakhi

What you need
Paper and art materials for writing and painting; Bhangra music.

Background
Baisakhi on 13 April is a happy joyful ceremony when Sikhs in India are able to celebrate their New Year and dance, sing and eat before they start the hard work of gathering the harvest. Sikhs all over the world remember it as the birthday of Guru Gobind Singh, who founded the Khalsa or Sikh brotherhood in 1699. For Sikh children there are several rites of passage. The first is when they are named as babies and Singh, meaning 'lion', is added to a boy's name and Kaur, meaning 'princess', is added to a girl's name. At the age of about 14 boys wear their first turban  and are allowed to join the Khalsa started by Guru Gobind Singh. To join the Khalsa, they will have to follow what is known as the five Ks. These are: uncut hair as a mark of holiness; a small wooden comb in the hair for cleanliness; a steel bracelet to remind them that they are connected to God; short cotton underwear (more practical than traditional Indian dress) and a Kirpan or small symbolic dagger for bravery.

What to do
● Talk to the children and discuss the background to the festival. Introduce them to the sound of Bhangra music with its hypnotic beat.
● Remind the children that this is another festival linked to harvest and ask them if they remember any others.
● The Khalsa is about joining and belonging. Talk about what they belong to. They should mention such things as families, their class, their school, football teams, sports clubs, Cubs, Brownies, maybe their church as well.
● Ask the children why it is good to belong to something. How does it make them feel?
● Let them write about their thoughts and feelings about belonging and use it a as part of a display.
● They could illustrate the organisations they belong to by painting their teams, their class or their Brownie or Cub six.

Differentiation
More able children can research more about how this festival is celebrated. Less able children will need support in the writing.

AGE RANGE 7–11

LEARNING OBJECTIVES
To understand why there is a need for this special day and to identify ways of celebrating it.

CURRICULUM LINKS
Geography: QCA Unit 8 'Improving the environment' – to think about how people affect the environment; Unit 24 'Passport to the world' – to understand that places are linked to other places in the world, to record and collect information about places, to investigate ways in which places are linked.

Earth Day

What you need
Map of the world; packaging from food items that the children have eaten recently – including cardboard, plastic bottles and tins.

Background
Earth Day is held on 22 April each year and is a time to look at the kinds of actions which are needed to help the environment. These will include preventing pollution, not wasting materials and being aware that many of the Earth's resources, such as forests, oil, coal and gas, are not renewable. Two useful websites are: www.getgreen.com and www.worldwildlife.org

What to do
● Talk about the background to Earth Day and start looking at what the children know about some of the global environmental issues. What do they think they can do as individuals to make the Earth a better place? For example, not wasting fuel or water, recycling, planting trees.
● Relate some of their ideas to what is happening locally. If possible visit the local recycling centre.
● Once you have built up a collection of packaging, discuss what can be recycled locally.
● Discuss what the packaging is made of and where it comes from (for example: paper from wood, plastics from oil, glass from sand).
● Look at the ingredients on the food labels. Where do they come from? Are they from England, Europe, or the rest of the world?
● Ask the children how the ingredients got to this country to be made into food and discuss the use of fuels to transport them, such as oil. Talk about eating seasonal and locally produced food. Would they want to stop eating some of the foods they take for granted?
● Discuss how the ingredients are converted into the finished product, for example, gas and electricity for cooking.
● What happens to the different types of packaging in their houses when they have used the products? This should bring back the idea of local recycling projects.

Differentiation
Less able children will need help in reading the food labels and matching the ingredients to different countries. More able children could use the world map and run cotton threads from different countries to labels with different foods on them, such as: tomatoes from Spain; winter apples from New Zealand.

AGE RANGE 5–11

LEARNING OBJECTIVES
To understand more about the background to Pesach and how it is celebrated.

CURRICULUM LINKS
Religious education: QCA Unit 1E 'How do Jewish people express theirs beliefs in practice?' – to learn about the key features of the story of the festival of Pesach; KS2 1b – to describe the variety of practices and ways of life in religions and understand how these stem from, and are closely connected, to beliefs and teachings.

Pesach (Passover)

What you need
Copies of 'Seder plate' photocopiable page 79;
11 large pieces of paper; other different coloured art paper; fabrics; paints and pastels; matzohs to eat.

Background
The Jewish festival of Pesach, or Passover, is held in April and celebrates the escape of the Jewish people from Egypt 3000 years ago. At this time the Israelites (Jewish people) were slaves of the Egyptians. Moses was instructed by God to go to the pharaoh and demand his people's freedom but he was ignored. Moses warned the pharaoh that God would send down severe punishment but again he was ignored. God sent a series of ten plagues. After the last plague, Pharaoh finally agreed

to Moses' request and the Israelites left their homes so quickly that there was not even time to bake their bread. They packed the raw dough to take with them and made it into flat hard crackers called matzohs, which are eaten during Pesach. Pharaoh then suddenly changed his mind and sent his army to chase Moses through the desert to the Red Sea. When the Israelites reached the sea they were trapped but the waters parted and let them cross into the promised land of Israel. As Pharaoh's army tried to follow, the waves closed in on them and swept it away. Pesach celebrates this history with an eight-day holiday. On the first two nights there are lavish meals called Seders.

What to do
● Tell the children about the background to Pesach. Explain that at the beginning of the festival of Pesach, Jewish families come together for a celebratory dinner called the Seder meal.
● Show the children the Seder plate photocopiable sheet. Explain to the children that in every Jewish home at the beginning of Pesach, you will find a Seder plate which holds the symbolic foods that are eaten during this time. These include shankbone, charoset, bitter herbs, parsley, salt water and roasted egg. Each food is there as a reminder of when the Jews were slaves and Moses led them to freedom.
● Tell the children that you would like them to find out, using the internet or information books, the special foods which are eaten at the beginning of Pesach. The children should then draw or write what they are on the Seder plate outline.
● Use the Seder plates as a base for a larger display.

Differentiation
Encourage more able children to find out what each symbolic food represents, for example, the bitter herbs are a reminder of the bitter times in slavery. Younger children could simply draw the special foods on to the Seder plate outline.

AGE RANGE 5–11

LEARNING OBJECTIVES
To understand more about who St George was and the way that 'good' triumphs over 'evil'.

CURRICULUM LINKS
NLS: Y2 T3 Text 20 – to write non-fiction texts, using texts read as models for own writing; Y4 T1 Text 23 – to write a newspaper-style report.
PSHE and citizenship: KS1 2c – to recognise the difference between right and wrong; KS2 2e – to reflect on spiritual, moral, social and cultural issues.

St George's Day

What you need
A longer account of St George and the Dragon – see: www.bbc.co.uk/religion/religions/christianity/features/stgeorge/index.shtml and www.bbc.co.uk/history/historic_figures/george_st.shtml; scrap paper; writing paper; paper and art materials to make posters.

Background
St George is the patron saint of England and St George's Day is 23 April. The flag of St George is a red cross on a white background. During the Crusades, the English army saw St George in a vision just before a battle which they won and Richard the Lionheart brought the flag to England. It is thought that St George was born somewhere in the Middle East, probably Turkey, and was a Roman soldier. He protested about the way the Romans were persecuting the Christians and was killed for his beliefs. The most famous story about St George is his fight with a dragon. The legend describes a town which was being terrorised by a dragon and a young princess was offered as a sacrifice. When George heard this he went to the town, killed the dragon and rescued the princess. It is unlikely that he ever fought a dragon and even less likely that he ever visited England. But in the Middle Ages the dragon was a symbol of the devil so the story is also about good triumphing over evil.

What to do
● Discuss the background to St George's Day and read the children a longer version of the fight with the dragon.
● Ask the children to imagine they are newspaper reporters. The editor has sent them to get the story about killing the dragon. The headline is already decided: DRAGON KILLED – GIRL RESCUED.
● They have to write a report of about 200 to 250 words so they might need to make notes and then draft the story for the right word length.
● Talk to the children about 'good' versus 'evil'. Make a list of bad things that need stopping at school or at home, such as bullying, fighting, litter, smoking or junk food.
● Ask them to make a poster showing St George defeating one of these 'evils'.

Differentiation
Less able children may find the writing difficult and will need support or they could just do the posters.

AGE RANGE 5–7

LEARNING OBJECTIVES
To understand more about some of the ways May Day is celebrated.

CURRICULUM LINKS
Science: QCA Unit 1B 'Growing plants' – to recognise that plants are living and need water and light to grow well; Unit 2B 'Plants and animals in the local environment' – to know that flowering plants produce seeds which grow into new plants.

May Day

What you need
Fruit and flowers to decorate the classroom; quick growing seeds such as mustard and cress, peas, broad beans and runner beans; plant pots or other containers; compost.

Background
The first day of the month of May is known as May Day and the first Monday is now a national holiday. It is when the weather begins to get warmer and flowers start to grow. Many people celebrate with lots of joyful and happy customs that celebrate the start of summer.

May Day as a festival of early summer probably started with the Roman festival of Flora, who was the goddess of fruit and flowers. Houses and whole villages were decorated with leaves and flowers to bring good fortune.

In the Middle Ages May Day was a favourite holiday and people used to cut down young trees, stick them in the ground and then dance round them to celebrate the fine weather that would allow planting to begin. Young girls would wash their faces with early morning dew to make them beautiful and young men would have archery competitions. Maypole dancing still takes place in some schools and in some villages. The original maypoles were freshly cut down trees that had been stripped of all their branches. In some villages there is also morris dancing, using ribbons, sticks and bells.

What to do
● Discuss the background to May Day with the children and talk to them about all the different celebrations.
● Ask them about the kinds of events and special days that they celebrate, such as birthdays and anniversaries, and ask what they do on these special days.
● Show the children the fruit and flowers that decorate the classroom. Remind them about May Day celebrating the summer and how farmers were able to start planting their seeds.
● Put the children into pairs to plant the seeds. If mustard and cress are used they can be eaten as an example of a quick crop (check with parents and carers first for any food allergies or dietary requirements).
● If peas and broad beans are used, they can be measured as they grow over a period of weeks and made to climb canes.

Differentiation
More able children can write about some of the May Day customs and do further research into the subject.

AGE RANGE 7–11

LEARNING OBJECTIVES
To understand more about what the Red Cross stands for and to learn about one of its important activities in the past.

CURRICULUM LINKS
History: KS2 2a – to learn about the characteristic features of the periods studied (the Second World War), including the experiences of men, women and children in the past.
Science: QCA Unit 5A 'Keeping healthy' – to recognise that a balanced and varied diet is needed to keep healthy.

World Red Cross Day

What you need
Paper and pencils.

Background
World Red Cross and Red Crescent Day, on 8 May, aims to bring attention to what the organisation does in countries all over the world and how important it is. The Red Cross was founded in 1863 and provides assistance to people who are affected by wars, violence and natural disasters. Wherever in the world there are people suffering, the Red Cross works to bring them food, water, shelter and medical treatment. It is able to work all over the world and will help both sides in any war. This is because it is a neutral and independent organisation which never, ever takes sides. The International Red Cross and Red Crescent Movement is the world's largest humanitarian network.

What to do
● Talk to the children about the work of the Red Cross and Red Crescent. Ask them where in the world they think the Red Cross is working now and what it is needed for.
● Ask the children what they think being 'neutral' means. Why do they think it is a good idea for the Red Cross and Red Crescent to be neutral?
● The Red Cross sent food parcels to soldiers captured in the Second World War. Each item was chosen to provide a good diet and 163,000 were sent once each week to all prisoners of war.
● Ask the children to work in groups and to choose 15 items to put in a food parcel. Remind them that the food would have to survive long, bumpy, hot journeys.
● Discuss which of their choices would be the best and show them the list of items below that went into the original Second World War parcels.

1. Packet of tea
2. Tin of cocoa
3. Bar of chocolate
4. Tinned sponge pudding
5. Tinned meat
6. Tin of processed cheese
7. Tin of condensed milk
8. Bar of soap
9. Tin of dried eggs
10. Tin of sardines
11. Tin of jam
12. Tin of margarine
13. Tin of sugar
14. Tin of vegetables
15. Tin of biscuits

● Discuss how the choices are different and talk about which ones are the best and why.

Differentiation
More able children could look at newspapers and the internet to find out exactly where the Red Cross is working. Less able children will need help with their lists.

AGE RANGE 5–11

LEARNING OBJECTIVES
To understand the reasons why Wesak is an important festival and to consider how it is celebrated.

CURRICULUM LINKS
Religious education: KS1 1d – to explore how religious beliefs and ideas can be expressed through the arts; 2a – to reflect on and consider religious and spiritual feelings; KS2 1b – to describe the variety of practices and ways of life in religions and understand how these stem from, and are closely connected, to beliefs and teachings.

Wesak

What you need
White paper; glue, bright paints, glitter and/or sequins; copies of 'Making a mandala' photocopiable page 80 and 'Vegetable parathas' photocopiable page 81; ingredients to make vegetable parathas.

Background
Wesak is the most important of the Buddhist festivals and takes place at the full moon in May. It celebrates the three important stages in the Buddha's life: his birthday, his 'enlightenment' when he learned the truth about life and how to avoid suffering and, for some Buddhists, it also marks his death. The celebrations last three days and houses are cleaned and decorated with flowers, candles and lanterns. There are processions in the street and many Buddhists will go to the temple and give offerings to the monks. If there is food, it will always be vegetarian because Buddhists try not to harm any living creature and believe that everyone should be able to live in harmony together.

What to do
● Talk about the background to Wesak and ask the children what they think it means to live in harmony together.
● What would make the school a better place for everyone to work together? It would be helpful to make a list and to try and do some of the things on it.
● Talk about what would need to happen to make the world a better place for everyone to live in harmony.
● Many Buddhists like bright colours, believing that they symbolise different parts of the mind. A circle called a mandala is used as an aid to concentration and to help the mind reach enlightenment.
● Use the photocopiable sheet to help the children make their own mandalas and display these around the classroom.
● Talk about what being a vegetarian means. If there are vegetarians in the class discuss what they eat instead of meat and fish.
● Make the vegetable parathas, using the photocopiable sheet, and enjoy eating them together, ensuring to check for any food allergies or dietary requirements beforehand.

Differentiation
The mandala circles are difficult and many children will need help in drawing the patterns. More able children could write about the life of Buddha and display this alongside the mandalas.

Interview sheet

This sheet can be used to interview grandmothers, mothers or aunts.
Ask them each question and make notes of their answers.

- Were you encouraged to do what you wanted?

_____

_____

- Did you have the same choices as men such as your brothers?

_____

_____

- Were you expected to get a certain kind of job?

_____

_____

- Have you had the same opportunities as men?

_____

_____

- For example, have you been paid the same?

_____

_____

- What sort of choices would you like girls in your family to have that you didn't have?

_____

_____

The story of Purim

Many years ago King Ahasuerus, the King of Persia, went looking for a wife. One day he saw a young girl called Esther. She was a beautiful orphan who was looked after by a Jewish man called Mordecai. The king was enchanted by Esther's beauty and cleverness and chose her to be his wife. However, Mordecai warned Esther that she must not tell the king that she was Jewish.

One day Mordecai was walking in the palace when he heard two guards planning to kill the king. He told Esther and she told her husband. The two men were arrested and Mordecai became famous as the man who had saved the king's life.

A few years later, the king appointed a new chief minister called Haman. Haman was filled with importance and told everyone that they should bow before him, however, Mordecai refused. Haman was furious and decided to find out everything about Mordecai. He discovered that Mordecai was Jewish and told the king that the Jews were plotting against him. The king trusted Haman, so he thought that it must be true. Haman decided upon a date when all the Jews would be killed – the thirteenth day of the twelfth month.

Mordecai sent word to Esther and begged her to save the Jews. She hadn't told the king that she was Jewish herself but she thought that she could change his mind. She went to see Mordecai and they worked out a plan. They told all the Jews not to eat and drink for three days and Esther agreed to do the same.

The next night Esther invited Haman and the king to a feast. As he was leaving he saw Mordecai who still wouldn't bow, and Haman was angry again. The next night Haman and the king were invited to another feast. Esther ate nothing but the king ate so much he couldn't sleep. While he tossed and turned he remembered that Mordecai had saved his life but had not been given many gifts. The next day the king asked Haman how he should reward someone who had pleased him. Haman thought that the king was talking about him so he told the king to give the man fine clothes and a royal horse. The next night Esther invited Haman and the King to a third banquet. The king told Haman to give the robe and the horse to the Mordecai. Haman was even more furious than ever. The king turned to Esther and asked her what gift she wanted. She said to him that if he loved her, he must give her the lives of all her people and get rid of their enemy Haman. She told the king that she was Jewish and that Haman had deceived him and told him lies about the Jews. He agreed and ordered that Haman was to be killed and all the Jews spared.

Make your own gragger

What you need:

- A tube about the same size as the centre of a toilet roll; plain white paper and thin card; sticky tape such as masking tape; glue, paints, felt-tipped pens or crayons; dried peas or lentils.

What to do

- Place the end of the tube on to thin card and draw round it, then draw a circle that is about 1cm larger all round than the diameter of the tube. It doesn't need to be perfect. Cut it out. Repeat this for the other end of the tube.

- Now make several cuts into one of the larger circles – not too far – so that when you place the end of the tube on to the thin card you can bend the larger circle up and stick it on to the tube with tape. It must be a good fit with no holes or gaps.

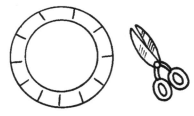 

- Fill the tube approximately one quarter full with dried peas or lentils and seal the other end by repeating the second instruction.
- At this stage it might look messy because of the masking tape; you need to use quite a lot to make a tight seal!
- Cut out some paper to fit around ends of the tube and stick it on with glue – not tape.
- Cut out some more paper and stick it round the tube with glue so that there is a good surface to paint and/or colour. When the glue is dry, make the gragger as colourful as possible and then check that it works!

What is special about my mum?

● Use the writing frame to tell everyone some of the things that are special about your mum.

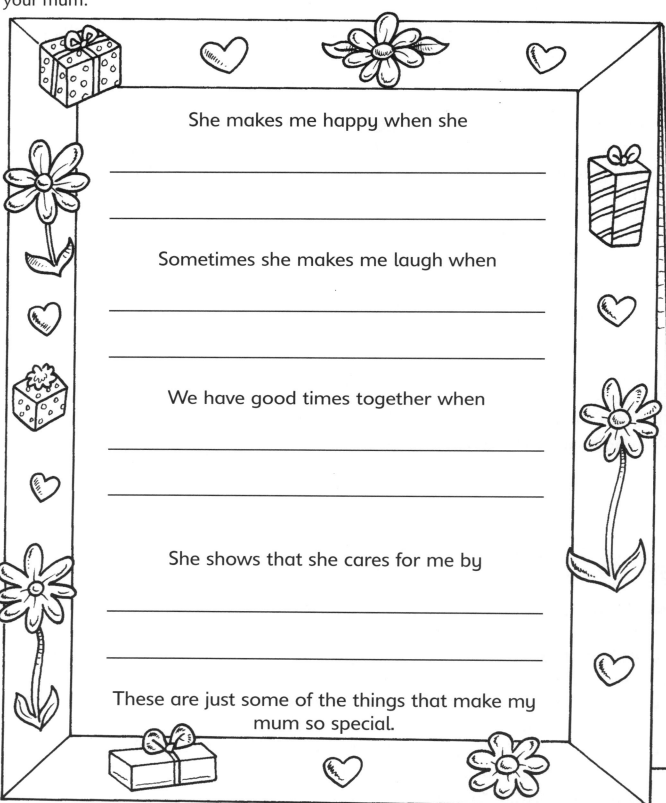

She makes me happy when she

_____

_____

Sometimes she makes me laugh when

_____

_____

_____

We have good times together when

_____

_____

She shows that she cares for me by

_____

_____

These are just some of the things that make my mum so special.

Festivals **BRIGHT IDEAS**

Balancing your food

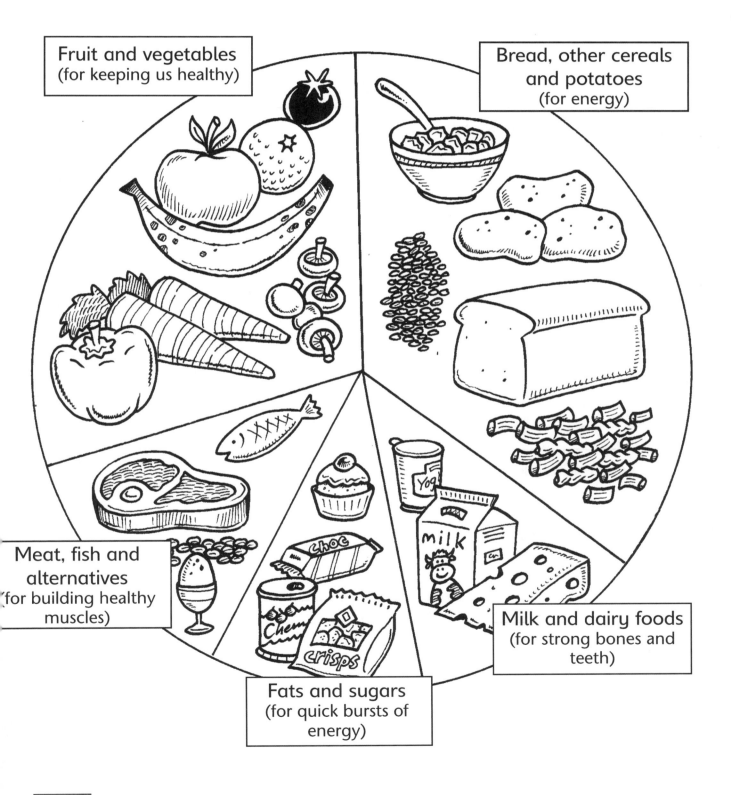

Fruit and vegetables
(for keeping us healthy)

Bread, other cereals
and potatoes
(for energy)

Meat, fish and
alternatives
(for building healthy
muscles)

Milk and dairy foods
(for strong bones and
teeth)

Fats and sugars
(for quick bursts of
energy)

Food groups

- Fruit and vegetables

- Bread, cereals and potatoes

- Meat, fish and alternatives

- Foods containing fats and/or sugar

- Milk and dairy products

Seder plate

Making a mandala

● Cut a large circle out of the white paper.

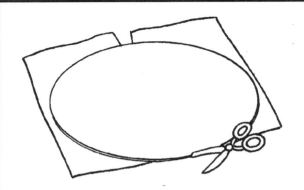

● Using a pair of compasses draw two concentric circles (see picture).

● Draw the flower pattern inside the inner circle.

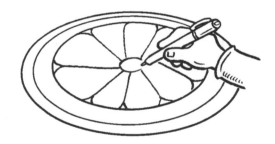

● Use the paints, glitter and sequins to make the mandala as brightly coloured as possible.

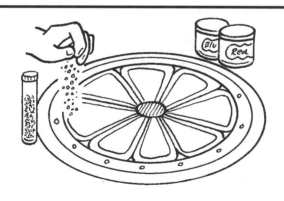

Vegetable parathas

Note: The parathas have to be fried in hot oil. This must be done by a responsible adult and not by a child. These instructions have been written in italics. Before cooking, please check the appropriate sections of the school's health and safety policy and make sure that appropriate risk assessments are available.

Ingredients (makes about 16)
450g plain wholemeal flour
120–175ml water
Melted butter or margarine
Grated raw cauliflower
Pinch of salt
Oil for frying

- Mix the flour and salt together and make a well in the centre.

- Slowly add enough water to make a soft dough and knead until it is no longer sticky.

- Divide the dough into 16 portions and roll each portion into a ball.

- Make a depression in the middle of each one and press a teaspoon of the grated cauliflower into the depression. Reshape the dough into a ball to enclose the filling.

- Carefully roll out each one into a circle of about 8cm.

- *Gently heat some oil in a frying pan and cook each paratha for approximately two minutes on each side, then add a teaspoon of butter or margarine and let it melt over the surface. Turn and cook until each paratha is golden brown on each side.*

- Cook all the parathas and stack them on top of each other in a clean tea towel.

CHAPTER 4

Summer
June to August

AGE RANGE 7–11

LEARNING OBJECTIVES:
To understand more about the Christian festival of Pentecost and some of its traditions and meanings.

CURRICULUM LINKS
Religious education: QCA Unit 4C 'Why is Easter important to Christians?' – to think about why Christians believe in life after death.
PSHE and citizenship: KS2 2k – to explore how the media present information.
NLS: Y4 T3 Text 25 – to design an advertisement.

Pentecost – Whitsuntide

What you need
Paper and pens for making posters; examples of good posters and adverts.

Background
Pentecost or Whitsuntide is celebrated on the Sunday that is the fiftieth day after Easter. Pentecost comes from a Greek word meaning 'fiftieth' and is thought originally to have been part of a Jewish harvest festival called Shavuot. Christians believe that Jesus had told the disciples that the Holy Spirit would appear to them and that they had to wait for this to happen. Fifty days after Jesus' resurrection from the dead (celebrated on Easter Sunday), the Holy Spirit came to the apostles as a hot wind with flickering fire and flames. (See Acts 2:1.) After this, the apostles started teaching people about Jesus and what they believed. Pentecost is celebrated as the start of the Christian church and is a favourite day for children to be christened. It is traditionally a time for walks and processions. Some towns in England roll cheeses down hills!

What to do
● Talk to the children about Pentecost and ask whether any of them go to church. If they do, ask them to describe what happens then to the rest of the class.
● Emphasise that Pentecost is the time when the disciples started telling the world about the Christian faith and how good it was.
● Ask the children to work in small groups and to talk about how they might try to persuade people that their school was the best one for children to come to. They should write down five of their best ideas to tell the class.
● Look at some of the posters and adverts together, and talk about advertising and information campaigns. What makes a good and persuasive poster? Look at the language and amount of text used, the balance of text to images and the type of images used.
● The children should work in pairs to design and complete a poster that tells everyone why their school is the best.

Differentiation
Less able children will need help with ideas for the written part of the poster. More able children could write down the complete list of why their school is the best.

AGE RANGE 7–11

LEARNING OBJECTIVES:
To recognise why the festival of Shavuot is celebrated and to understand how it is linked to some of our laws.

CURRICULUM LINKS
Religious education: KS2 1a – to describe the key aspects of a religion, especially the people, stories and traditions that influence the beliefs and values of others.
Citizenship: QCA Unit 8 'How do rules and laws affect me?' – to understand the importance of rules.

Shavuot

What you need
Paper for writing; copies of
'The Ten Commandments' photocopiable page 92; cheesecake to eat.

Background
Shavuot is a Jewish festival which always begins on the fiftieth day after the first day of the spring festival of Pesach. The Christian festival of Pentecost comes from Shavuot. It celebrates the wheat harvest and is also when God appeared and spoke to the people that Moses had led out of Egypt. The Israelites had wandered in the desert until they came to the foot of Mount Sinai which was covered with flowers and trees. They set up camp, bathed and washed their clothes. Three days later they were woken by thunder, lightning and thick dark clouds. They heard the sound of the ram's horn (shofar) and the earth trembled and shook. God spoke to them and gave them many laws, including the Ten Commandments.

The first night of the festival is spent praying and reading the holy book – the Torah. Synagogues and houses are decorated with branches, leaves and wreaths of roses. Another Shavuot custom is eating food with lots of milk and butter. Jews have many strict rules about food and eating and during the first Shavuot they had no cooking pots and were forced to eat only dairy foods. Today during the celebrations they eat blintzes and cheesecakes.

What to do
● Discuss the festival and emphasise that it was the time when God told Jewish people about their laws.
● Ask the children what laws they know about, such as those about theft, murder or violence, and minor laws to do with speeding and parking.
● Discuss what laws are for and why they should not be broken.
● Talk about school rules and ask them to work in small groups to make up their own Ten School Commandments. Each one should start with: 'You must…' or 'You must not…'
● Read each group's list to the class and write down the ten best ones to display.
● Read out and show them some of the Ten Commandments from photocopiable page 92.
● Talk about the similarities between the Ten Commandments and today's laws.
● Share out and eat the cheesecake.

Differentiation
More able children can find out more about kosher foods and many of the eating rules which Jews have to follow.

AGE RANGE 5–11

LEARNING OBJECTIVES:
To begin to develop an understanding of why it is important to think carefully about what we need to do to protect the environment.

CURRICULUM LINKS
Geography: KS1 5b – to recognise how the environment can be improved and sustained; QCA Unit 6 'Investigating our local area'; Unit 8 'Improving the environment' – to think about how people affect the environment.

World Environment Day

What you need
Paper and pencils for notes; writing paper.

Background
World Environment Day is celebrated on 5 June each year. Its main aim is to encourage people to become active in the kinds of environmental issues that will help all people in all countries to enjoy a safer and more prosperous future. Some of the environmental problems include the destruction of rain forests, the ozone layer, wildlife habitats, water, the greenhouse effect, air pollution and the use of fossil fuels.

What to do
● Discuss the background to World Environment Day with the children and find out what they think environmental problems actually are.
● Talk about what they can do to help, for example, not leaving the tap running, flushing the toilet less, walking rather than travelling by car, recycling rather than throwing away, growing and using local food.
● Ask the children to work in small groups and list what they will try to do for one day to help protect the environment.
● Remind them about these ideas:
   1.   have a shower instead of a bath and do not leave the tap running when you clean your teeth;
   2.   only boil as much water in the kettle as you need;
   3.   walk, cycle or share lifts in the car;
   4.   travel by train rather than plane;
   5.   reuse or take your own bags when you go to the supermarket;
   6.   use a compost bin at home to turn green waste into garden compost;
   7.   turn off the television and other electrical equipment – do not leave them on standby.
● Ask them to try one of their ideas for a day and then discuss how difficult or easy they found it.
● Ask the children to write about what they feel is the most important environmental issue, what they think should be done about it – and, of course what they can do.
● Mount these on the wall under the heading: 'How to save the world'.

Differentiation
Less able children could write one idea and one thing that they can do. More able children could concentrate on one area such as 'pollution' or 'energy conservation' and be given time to produce an in-depth study.

National School Grounds Week

AGE RANGE 5–11

LEARNING OBJECTIVES:
To help children understand the importance of their
school grounds and that they can be used in all kinds
of imaginative ways.

CURRICULUM LINKS
Geography: QCA Unit 1 'Around out school – the
local area' – to express views on the features of the
local environment; Unit 6 'Investigating our local
area'; Unit 8 'Improving the environment' – to think
about how people affect the environment.

What you need

Plans of the school; highlighter pens; drawing paper; copies of 'Seed planting plans'
photocopiable page 93; growbags and an area to use them (or a designated area of
ground); assorted vegetable and flower seeds.

Background

National School Grounds Week is an annual
celebration of school grounds that highlights
the importance and value of school grounds
for learning and play. It is organised
by Learning through Landscapes
and resource packs are available on
www.ltl.org.uk. It takes place in mid
June but needs planning well ahead
for planting and growing.

What to do

● With the children in groups, ask them
to look at the plans of the school and to
highlight hard areas and grass areas that are
used for play.
● Look at the plans and talk about areas that
could be used as gardens, for ponds or wildlife areas. If
your school already has these areas, highlight them in a different colour. If your school
has very little grass or flowerbeds, remind children about the use of containers and
growbags.
● Ask them to work in pairs and to design a new play area or a wildlife area. The
finished designs can be used as a display.
● Show them the packets of seeds that include peas, dwarf beans, lettuce, radishes,
spring onions and different varieties and colours of flowers. Discuss the growing
instructions.
● Ask them to work in pairs and give them the 'Seed planting plans' photocopiable
sheet. They must plan how they will plant their patch of ground or their growbag. They
can try several ways and then choose the one they feel will work.
● Plant the seeds in the growbags or ground making sure that the children's names are
clearly marked and the seeds labelled.
● Water them, get rid of weeds and watch them grow. During National School
Grounds Week, look at the ones that have grown the best. Talk about why they think
they have improved the school's grounds.

Differentiation

Less able children will need help with the plans and the 'Seed planting plans'
photocopiable sheet. More able children could research and write about reasons why
plants grow well and the reasons why they do not.

AGE RANGE 5–11

LEARNING OBJECTIVES
To learn more about the history of Father's Day and to recognise some of the important help that fathers give to children.

CURRICULUM LINKS
NLS: Y1 T3 Text 16 – to compose poetic sentences; Y2 T2 Text 15 – to write poems from initial jottings; Y3 T2 Text 15 – to write poetry that creates effects using sound; Y4 T3 Text 14 – to write poems, experimenting with different styles; Y6 T1 Text 10 – to produce revised poems for reading aloud.

Father's Day

What you need
Paper and pencils for notes; copies of 'Special day' photocopiable page 94.

Background
Father's Day is celebrated on the third Sunday in June and started in America. Mrs Dodd from Washington wanted a special day to honour her father, William Smart. Mrs Dodd's mother had died giving birth to her sixth child and Mr Smart was left to bring up all the children – including Mrs Dodd – on his own. It was after she became an adult that she realised how difficult it must have been for her father and how good he had been at looking after all the children. After the first Father's Day had been held in 1910, it began to be celebrated in a few other towns across America. In 1924 President Calvin Coolidge supported the idea of a national Father's Day and in 1966 President Lyndon Johnson declared the third Sunday in June as Father's Day.

When discussing the subject of fathers, remember that some children will not have fathers at home – for many different reasons – and so sensitivity will be required.

What to do
● Discuss the background to Father's Day and stress that compared to festivals such as Mothering Sunday it is a modern celebration.
● In groups, ask the children to identify an event or person they think is important and special enough to have a 'festival' day.
● As a class, choose the most popular. What kind of day would it be? When would the day occur? What kind of celebrations would take place? Would any special food be eaten or stories told?
● Talk about their reasons and ideas with the whole class and list all the popular ones on the whiteboard.
● Give each child the 'Special day' photocopiable sheet with the poem framework. Ask them to write a poem with each line starting with the appropriate letter and suggest the celebrations that they would like to have.
● The groups could also suggest what the food they would like to eat on their special day and could write out the menus. You could read these out and display them alongside the poems.

Differentiation
More able children should produce poems with lines that are several words long. Less able children will need a lot of support and need only use two or three words for each line.

Midsummer and the Summer Solstice

AGE RANGE 5–11

LEARNING OBJECTIVES:
To understand more about what the Summer Solstice is and to develop ideas about what summer actually means to children.

CURRICULUM LINKS
Science: KS1 Sc4.3a – to identify the Sun as a light source; KS2 Sc4.4b – to understand how the position of the Sun appears to change during the day, and how shadows change as this happens.

What you need

Writing paper; art paper and materials for collage.

Background

The word 'solstice' comes from the Latin *sol* meaning sun and *stice* to stand still. The Summer Solstice, which is around 21 June, marks the beginning of summer when the Sun reaches its highest point in the sky and makes it the longest day of the year. Many of the prehistoric stone circles such as Stonehenge were thought to have been built to worship the Sun.

Midsummer Day celebrations, on the 24 June, were part of Celtic fire festivals when fires were lit to represent the Sun. There are many traditions associated with Midsummer; for example, because it was thought to be a magical time, people would stay awake all night to avoid being taken away by fairies. Midsummer dew was thought to have healing powers and girls and older women would wash their faces in it to make themselves look younger and more beautiful. Plants and flowers were picked and burnt on the bonfires to protect crops and animals. Wearing your clothes inside out on Midsummer's Eve was thought to keep you out of trouble and danger for the next year. Young couples could pledge themselves to get married within a year and a day. The festival also became known as St John's Day and was an important celebration of the birth of St John the Baptist.

What to do

● Explain the background to Midsummer and the Summer Solstice to the children and emphasise that it began when people celebrated the Sun as a magical power that made growing crops and rearing animals possible.
● Ask them to discuss in groups what the Sun and summer means to them. This could be holidays, special days out, wearing favourite summer clothes, playing outdoors or going swimming.
● Working on their own, children should write about a special summer or a special holiday.
● Children could work in groups to do bright summer paintings or collages, using yellows, reds and blues.

Differentiation

More able children could find out more about summer festivals in other European countries. Less able children could concentrate on artwork and write one or two sentences about their special summer.

AGE RANGE 7–11

LEARNING OBJECTIVES:
To understand more about the problems faced as the population of the world increases.

CURRICULUM LINKS
PSHE and citizenship: KS2 2j – that resources can be allocated in different ways and that these economic choices affect individuals, communities and the sustainability of the environment.
Geography: KS2 5a – to recognise how people can improve the environment or damage it, and how decisions about places and environments affect the future quality of people's lives.

World Population Day

What you need
Class-lists with the number of children in the school and the numbers in each class.

Background
World Population Day is celebrated on 11 July. It is concerned with the number of people on Earth, how to improve everyone's quality of life and how to achieve a better future. The world's population currently stands at over 6 billion people and will grow during the next 40 years by at least another 1.5 billion. More than 90 per cent of this population growth is in the developing world, where food, water and other resources are scarce. Plants and animals are now becoming extinct at a rate which is 50 to 100 times faster than they naturally would because of the impact of more and more people.

What to do
● Ask the children what problems they think are caused by more and more people living in the world.
● Discuss what these large numbers of people need, such as food, water, houses and transport.
● Talk about the impact on wildlife and the problems of using more land to grow more food.
● Ask the children to work in groups and see if they can think of any solutions to the world's population problem. They may develop futuristic ideas, such as colonising other planets and living under the sea, as well as moral ideas such as stopping people having children.
● Give each group the class-lists, showing the numbers of children in each class.
● What do they think will happen if five or ten more children arrive in the school? They should be able to say that they could be divided quite easily amongst the classes.
● What would happen if 100 new children arrive? Discuss the need for new classrooms and more school meals. Where would new classrooms be built? Would the school be a better place?
● Tell them to imagine that ten more children will be arriving in their class tomorrow. What problems will have to be solved?

Differentiation
More able children can do further research into the maths of population growth by looking at the figures for their local town or area.

AGE RANGE 5–11

LEARNING OBJECTIVES:
To learn more about weather sayings and whether they are ever true.

CURRICULUM LINKS
Geography: KS1 4a – to make observations about features in the environment, such as season changes in weather; KS2 4a – to recognise and explain patterns made by physical features in the environment.
Science: KS1 Sc1.1 – to collect evidence by making observation and measurements when answering a questions; KS2 Sc1.1a – to establish links between causes and effects.

St Swithin's Day

What you need
Copies of 'Weather sayings' photocopiable page 95; writing paper; art paper and materials; pine cones.

Background
St Swithin's Day is 15 July and the tradition is that whatever the weather is like on St Swithin's Day it will stay the same for the next 40 days:

'St Swithin's Day, if it does rain
Full 40 days it will remain
St Swithin's Day, if it be fair
For 40 days, t'will rain no more'.

St Swithin was the Saxon Bishop of Winchester and he had asked to be buried out of doors in the Sun and the rain. This happened, and for nine years his wishes were followed but then the monks of Winchester removed his remains into a beautiful shrine inside the cathedral. Legend says that there was a rainstorm during the ceremony and that it continued to rain for 40 days.

What to do
● Talk to the children about the legend of St Swithin's Day and ask them if they know any weather sayings. Write down any that are not on the 'Weather sayings' photocopiable sheet.
● Show the children the 'Weather sayings' photocopiable sheet and read through the sayings. Which ones do they think are true? Is it possible to prove that any of them are true?
● Choose some of the sayings to investigate. For example, tell them to look out for the next time it rains before 7 o'clock so they can check whether the rain stops before 11 o'clock. When there are a lot of squeaky chairs look to see whether it is raining. Do daisies close up before rain?
● Put pine cones on the classroom window sills. They are supposed to close up in damp weather. Do they?
● Research weather forecasting on the internet and find out how today's meteorologists forecast the weather – useful websites are: www.bbc.co.uk/weather/ and www.metoffice.gov.uk. If there is a weather station in school, all kinds of weather records can be kept and different weather sayings proved or disproved.
● Ask the children to work in pairs and to write a two-line weather saying of their own and mount these on the wall.
● Ask them to illustrate any one of the weather sayings as a cartoon.

Differentiation
Less able children will need help in thinking of a weather saying – this is a short but quite difficult activity.

The Birthday of Haile Selassi

What you need
CD player and reggae music, for example by Bob Marley; pictures of Haile Selassi; map of the world showing Ethiopia and Jamaica.

Background
Rastafarians take their name from Emperor Haile Selassi of Ethiopia, who was also known as Ras (which means prince) Tafari. The religious faith known as Rastafari is not a very old religion. It started in Jamaica in the 1920s and took its name when Haile Selassi was crowned emperor of Ethiopia in 1930. Rastafarians believe that he is descended from King Solomon in the Bible and is the incarnation of God. They also think that he will help black people – who can trace their ancestors back to the slave trade – to return to Africa. This is because Africa, and Ethiopia in particular, is the spiritual home of Rastafarianism. Haile Selassi was born on 23 July 1892 and his birthday is one of the holiest days of the year for Rastafarians.

What to do
● Show the children what Haile Selassi looked like and where Ethiopia and Jamaica are. During the discussion about Rastafarianism play some reggae music.
● Explain that music is very important to Rastafarians and that one of the most famous musicians was Bob Marley.
● Discuss the importance of Haile Selassi. Explain that many people now living in Jamaica and other Caribbean islands are there because their families had been taken by force from African countries many years before and made to work as slaves. Haile Selassi spoke up for black people who had suffered because of slavery. This is why Rastafarians believe that everyone is equal and that we should all speak out against situations where people are treated unfairly.
● Ask the children to work in groups and to think of a situation in school where they have seen someone treated unfairly or where they have treated someone unfairly.
● Ask one person from each group to be the spokesperson for their group and to explain their 'unfair situation' to the rest of the class.
● Ask each group to think of an unfair situation in the world and repeat the process.

Differentiation
More able pupils could do further research into what Rastafarians believe in.

Lammas Day

AGE RANGE 5–11

LEARNING OBJECTIVES:
To understand the meaning of Lammas Day and to have opportunities to think more about how people are able to live together happily.

CURRICULUM LINKS
Science: QCA Unit 1B 'Growing plants' – to name plants that we grow for food.
PSHE and citizenship: KS1 4d – to understand that family and friends should care for each other; KS2 4c – to develop the skills to be effective in relationships.

What you need
Paper and pencils; one sheet of large paper; bread (to share out); butter or margarine; spreads such as jam and honey.

Background
Lammas Day is 1 August and in Britain it was celebrated as the start of the harvest. The name Lammas probably comes from an Anglo-Saxon word *Hlaefmaesse* which means 'loaf mass'. It was when people went to church to celebrate the first corn to be cut in the fields. On Lammas Day farmers used the first corn to bake bread which they gave to their local church. The bread was then used as the Communion bread as part of a harvest festival. Some of the bread was also allowed to go stale and crumbled in the corners of the farmers' barns for good luck and future good harvests. Nowadays, harvest festivals are celebrated in late September. Another tradition was that on Lammas Day young people could agree to a 'trial marriage', lasting 11 days, to see whether they were really suited to be together. At the end of the 11 days, if they didn't get on with each other, they could part.

What to do
● Ask the children why celebrating the harvest was important and what would happen if there was a bad harvest.
● Explain that the corn is made into bread, which is one of the world's staple foods.
● Ask them what they think some of the other staple foods are; for example, rice, pasta, noodles and potatoes.
● Ask the children to think about the idea of friends and to list all the good things about their friends.
● Remind the children about the 'trial marriage' to see whether people can get on with each other. Ask them to list all the characteristics that they think make a friend easy to get on with.
● Read out as many of these 'characteristics' as possible and write the six most important on a large piece of paper headed 'How to be friends'.
● Remind the children that Lammas Day celebrates the first corn and that corn provides us with bread.
● Share out the bread and butter and enjoy it.

Differentiation
Less able children will need help with writing down the characteristics that help people get on with each other. Perhaps they could say what they think and a teaching assistant could write it down.

The Ten Commandments

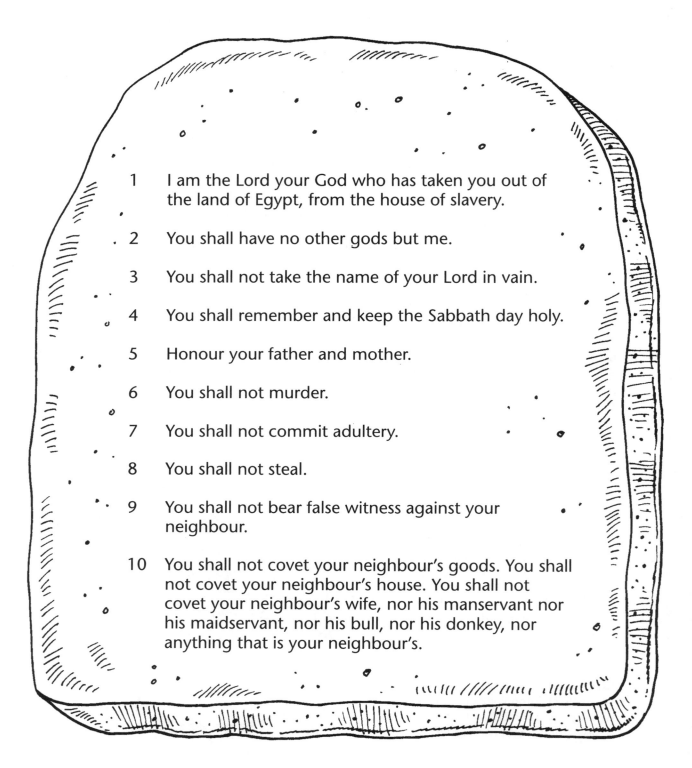

1   I am the Lord your God who has taken you out of the land of Egypt, from the house of slavery.

2   You shall have no other gods but me.

3   You shall not take the name of your Lord in vain.

4   You shall remember and keep the Sabbath day holy.

5   Honour your father and mother.

6   You shall not murder.

7   You shall not commit adultery.

8   You shall not steal.

9   You shall not bear false witness against your neighbour.

10   You shall not covet your neighbour's goods. You shall not covet your neighbour's house. You shall not covet your neighbour's wife, nor his manservant nor his maidservant, nor his bull, nor his donkey, nor anything that is your neighbour's.

Note: Because Shavuot is a Jewish celebration these Ten Commandments are the Jewish interpretation. Different religions have different versions.

Seed planting plans

There are three plans so that you can try different planting designs. Remember, the ground or the growbag that you have available is about 1m by 40cm.

PLAN 1 Vegetables
Growing tips to think about: How many different vegetables do you want to grow? Where should the tallest ones be planted? How close together will your plants be?

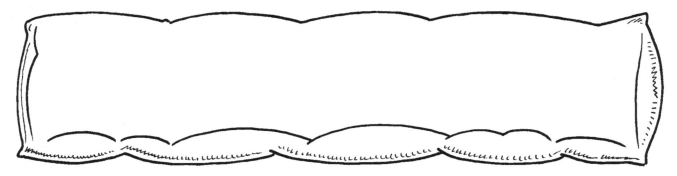

PLAN 2 Vegetables and flowers
Growing tips to think about: Are you going to mix the seeds up so flowers grow among the vegetables? Or are you going to grow them in separate patches of ground? Which plants should be at the front? How close together can you plant them?

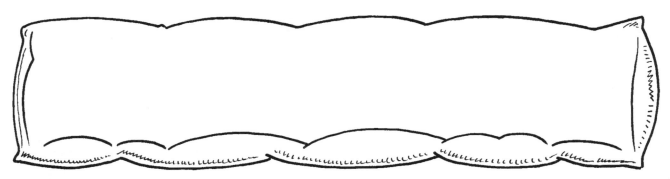

PLAN 3 Flowers
Growing tips to think about: It will be a good idea to use colour and plan where flowers of different colours are going to be planted. Make sure you know which of the flowers are the tallest and which the smallest.

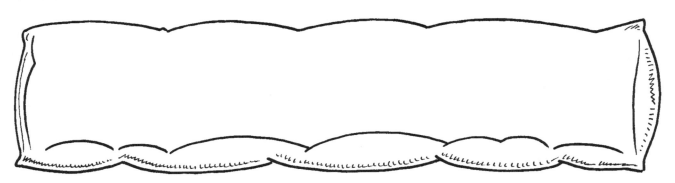

Special day

My special day celebrates

_____

It is celebrated on

_____

I have decided to make this a special day because

_____

_____

On this day people

_____

_____

SPECIAL DAY

S _____

P _____

E _____

C _____

I _____

A _____

L _____

D _____

A _____

Y _____

Festivals **BRIGHT IDEAS**

Weather sayings

Red sky at night sailor's delight.

Red sky in the morning, sailor's warning.

Rain before seven fine for eleven.

Snow is due when the cat washes behind both ears.

Cows lying down means wet weather – cows standing up means fine weather.

When chairs squeak it is of rain they speak.

Cast not a clout till May be out
(don't change from your winter clothes until the end of May).

Lots of berries on the trees means a bad winter.

Rooks building high nests means a mild winter –
rooks building low nests means a stormy winter.

The daisy shuts its eye before rain.

Available in this series:

ISBN 0-439-97131-4
978-0439-97131-7

ISBN 0-439-97132-2
978-0439-97132-4

ISBN 0-439-97133-0
978-0439-97133-1

ISBN 0-439-97135-7
978-0439-97135-5

ISBN 0-439-97175-6
978-0439-97175-1

ISBN 0-439-97176-4
978-0439-97176-8

ISBN 0-439-96503-9
978-0439-96503-3

ISBN 0-439-96511-X
978-0439-96511-8

ISBN 0-439-94487-2
978-0439-94487-8

ISBN 0-439-96541-1
978-0439-96541-5

To find out more, call: 0845 603 9091
or visit our website www.scholastic.co.uk